"*Life-Changing Mission* is on a short-term mission trip. Packed with real stories from missionaries and powerful insights from the book of Acts, it will help you grow closer to God and give you the courage to make a lasting impact as you serve others. Get ready to experience something truly life-changing!"

Neil Powell, Redeemer City to City; co-director, The London Project; author of *Together for the City*

"This resource has no posing or pretending but contains real stories of how the lyric, music, and dance of the gospel has compelled my friends at Serge to live, long, and love to the glory of God among the nations of the world. I am grateful to call this family of missionaries my family. Their tears and hope are mine."

Scotty Smith, Pastor Emeritus, Christ Community Church, Franklin, TN; teacher-in-residence, West End Community Church, Nashville, TN

"As a person who has led more than fifty short-term mission trips, I would highly recommend this book for your short-term mission team, particularly the daily devotions for when you are on the field. Each devotion is based in Scripture, with both biblical truth and personal stories interwoven into each day's reading. They also give the reader room for personal reflection each day to process how God has revealed himself during that day's work. This is a highly useful tool for short-term mission teams."

Danny Kwon, Senior Director of Youth Ministry Content and Cross-Cultural Initiatives, Rooted Ministry

"*Life-Changing Mission* is a great resource for those going on short-term mission trips. The book is full of timely, relevant, and insightful reflections on passages from the book of Acts, written by experienced missionaries. I highly recommend it!"

Lloyd Kim, Coordinator, Mission to the World

"Short-term mission trips have the potential to range from okay to life-changing. It's when we experience God and have a sense of how he is at work in and through us that mission trips have the ability to move the needle of our lives dramatically. This devotional seeks to do that very thing—to connect us to God and his grace for us and to send us on his mission to bring his love into his world."

Chad Brewer, Coordinator, RUF International and RUF Global

"*Life-Changing Mission* by Serge is an inspiring guide for anyone embarking on a short-term trip. With heartfelt, gospel-centered devotions, this book transforms travel into a meaningful journey. It is written from years of experience and a deep love for God's mission. This book is a comprehensive spiritual resource, making it an essential companion for your next mission trip!"

Robert Kim, Philip and Rebecca Douglass Chair of Church Planting and Christian Formation, associate professor, Covenant Theological Seminary

LIFE-CHANGING MISSION

Devotions for Your Short-Term Trip

Patric Knaak, Editor

New
Growth
Press

newgrowthpress.com

New Growth Press, Greensboro, NC 27401
newgrowthpress.com
Copyright © 2024 by Patric Knaak

Scripture quotations are taken from THE HOLY BIBLE, NEW INTERNATIONAL VERSION®, NIV® Copyright © 1973, 1978, 1984, 2011 by Biblica, Inc.® Used by permission. All rights reserved worldwide.

Cover Design: Faceout Books, faceoutstudio.com
Interior Typesetting and eBook: Lisa Parnell, lparnellbookservices.com

ISBN: 978-1-64507-487-8 (paperback)
ISBN: 978-1-64507-488-5 (ebook)

Printed in the United States of America

29 28 27 26 25   1 2 3 4 5

CONTENTS

After the Trip

BEFORE YOU GO
Introduction: It's Not Over Yet

BY PATRIC KNAAK

There was no indication that this neighborhood was any different from the blocks surrounding it. But as I rounded the corner, the close-packed stone buildings abruptly gave way to the sprawling grounds of a ruined, ancient church. And there on the edge of the site was a five-foot-tall, nearly white, marble pillar. As I stood before it, I was overcome with emotion as I realized that the apostle Paul had also stood here.

Acts 13 details the start of Paul's first missionary journey. Commissioned by the elders of the church in Antioch, Paul and Barnabas were sent off to preach the gospel, and their first stop was Barnabas's home island of Cyprus (Acts 13:1–3). As they preached their way across the island, they eventually ended up in the western port city of Paphos where Paul was opposed by a Jewish sorcerer, Elymas (Acts 13:4–12). Scripture records the details of the confrontation between Paul and Elymas, ending with Elymas being temporarily blinded by the power of the Holy Spirit for opposing Paul. But church history also tells us that as part of their confrontation, Elymas had Paul bound and whipped.

As I stood on that street in Paphos, looking at the very marble pillar to which Paul had been chained, I had a deep sense of being part of something much larger. I was on Cyprus to lead a retreat for a team of fellow missionaries, and yet I was standing on the same ground that Paul and Barnabas had tread. Even though the *events* of the book of Acts have ended, its *story* has not. The story of the expansion of God's kingdom continues today. And you and I are part of it, every bit as much as Paul and Barnabas were.

Life-Changing Mission was written to help you connect deeply with your heavenly Father as you join his "family business" of seeing his kingdom expand. God is at work using weak and broken people to bring the message of his good news to those who do not yet know him. We've rooted each of our devotions in the book of Acts because God still

- transforms scared people like Peter to become bold witnesses for him (compare Luke 22:54–62 with Acts 2:14–41),
- works in our suffering to bring about his glory, just as he did when Stephen was stoned (Acts 7),
- draws the most unlikely of people to himself through the most unlikely means, as he did with the Ethiopian eunuch (Acts 8) and Paul (Acts 9), and
- breaks down barriers like those between Peter and Cornelius that humanly speaking seem impenetrable (Acts 10).

The book of Acts focuses on the work and role of the Holy Spirit in our lives. God the Father establishes the plan for our salvation and the renewal of our broken world. God the Son carries out that plan through his coming, living, dying, and rising again. But it is God the Holy Spirit who makes that plan effective in our lives as he regenerates and indwells us, and then empowers us to live on mission.

Mission trips give us a unique opportunity to see and experience God differently than we do at home. Away from the demands of "normal" life, things come into focus differently. Our need for God's provision is more evident. Jesus's words echo a little more clearly. God's passion to see others redeemed is on display.

You'll notice that all of the devotions in *Life-Changing Mission* are written by our missionaries at Serge. They are men and women who have given their lives to seeing God's kingdom come. They are also some of my favorite people in the world because, as you'll see, they have no illusion of being "super Christians." They are people who know that they need Jesus's grace each and every day of their lives in order to follow him.

Our prayer for you isn't simply that you'll have a good trip—though we do want that. Rather, it is that you will taste God's kingdom firsthand and then live every day differently because your mission trip was truly life-changing.

Patric Knaak, Deputy Director of Mission, Serge

HOW TO GET THE MOST OUT OF *LIFE-CHANGING MISSION*

Life-Changing Mission is designed to be a comprehensive spiritual resource for your short-term mission trip. At the heart of *Life-Changing Mission* are ten daily devotions specifically written for individuals and teams participating in short-term mission work. But *Life-Changing Mission* also contains material to help you prepare for and debrief after your trip, includes travel features to give you a place to record the details and memories of your adventure, offers additional ideas for devotionals and journaling, and contains lots of space to let you capture your experiences and conversations with God.

BEFORE YOU GO

INTRODUCTION
A basic introduction to *Life-Changing Mission* and an overview of its features.

PRE-TRIP EXERCISE: READY OR NOT?
Designed to help you identify some of your needs and hopes going into the trip, Ready or Not? will also give you the chance to journal about things you'd like to see God do on your trip and to craft a prayer update to send out before you leave.

TRAVELOGUE FEATURES: MY TEAMMATES; HOLDING THE ROPES
My Teammates and Holding the Ropes provide easy ways to record the names and contact information for your teammates and your supporters.

ON THE TRIP
DAILY DEVOTIONS

Life-Changing Mission's daily devotions are designed to help you connect with Christ in deep and refreshing ways as you experience the highs and lows of your journey. Every day begins with a passage from Acts that focuses on the Holy Spirit's work advancing Jesus's mission in the world. A brief article, each written by a different Serge missionary, provides the content for each day and is followed by thought-provoking questions and prayer and journaling exercises. Each devotion also includes a reflection section where you can record how you saw God work during the course of the day. Because they can be completed in thirty minutes, the devotions are easy to schedule consistently throughout your trip.

ADDITIONAL DEVOTIONAL RESOURCE: INTRODUCING *LECTIO DIVINA*

For trips lasting longer than ten days, the Additional Devotional Resource section on page 99 will help you use an ancient method of devotional reading that combines Scripture and prayer into an intimate listening experience with God.

TRAVELOGUE FEATURES: OUR JOURNEY; TRAVEL MEMORIES; NEW FRIENDS; MISSION MEMORIES; BY THE NUMBERS

Our Journey, New Friends, Mission Memories, and By the Numbers all provide handy ways to record the unique memories, people, and experiences you'll encounter along the way.

AFTER THE TRIP

God's work in your life doesn't end when you return home. In many ways, it's just beginning. To help you make the lessons of your trip last a lifetime, the debrief exercises will help you record and organize your thoughts, listen more intently to God, and discern his plans for you as you think about the future. They will also help you continue to live *on mission*—with the same outward focus of helping others meet Jesus that you developed during your trip.

DEBRIEF ONE: MAKING SENSE OF WHAT YOU'VE SEEN

Completed on your journey home or in the first week after you're back, the first debrief will help you to record the spiritual lessons of your trip while they are fresh and to reflect on all the ways that God was at work during your trip. It will also help you prepare to tell your story to your church, friends, and supporters.

DEBRIEF TWO: THE GOSPEL IN AND THROUGH YOU TO OTHERS

Completed four to six weeks after you're back and the dust has settled, the second debrief is geared toward helping you connect the experiences and lessons of your trip with your daily life. It features a planning section designed to help you come up with some concrete ways to live more missionally—to pray, serve, give, and go in ways that will help others see Jesus more clearly—as part of your normal lifestyle.

DEBRIEF THREE: THE ONGOING JOURNEY

Completed six months after your trip, the final debrief will help you review your plans and consider additional ways to be missionally engaged, involved in helping God's kingdom grow and new people find Christ.

CONCLUSION: WRITING THE NEXT CHAPTER

Final thoughts to help you keep living your own life-changing mission.

PRE-TRIP EXERCISE
Ready or Not?

To be done one week pre-trip

As you prepare to leave for your mission trip in the next week, it's likely that you are feeling a wide range of emotions. Often, getting ready to do ministry in a different cultural context can bring out strange paradoxes in our hearts. We can, at the exact same moment, feel both excited about what God will do in and through us and yet slightly panicked at the hundreds of unknowns that lie ahead. If you're feeling this spectrum of emotion this week, you're in good company!

PART 1: INVENTORY OF NEEDS AND HOPES

Take a few minutes in the busyness of packing and checking off your pre-trip to-do list to take an inventory of your needs and hopes for your trip. Then answer the questions below.

I am AFRAID of

☐ the unknown

☐ entering an unknown culture or situation

☐ being away from family and home

☐ having to do things that will be hard

☐ being asked to eat "disgusting" food

☐ not knowing what I'm doing

☐ feeling unprepared or incapable

☐ making mistakes/making others angry

☐ getting hurt or sick

☐ my prayers not being answered

☐ my family getting hurt or sick while I'm gone

☐ not having enough privacy or down time

I feel UNDER PRESSURE to

☐ not let others see my sin and fears

☐ be perfect (or cover it up if I'm not)

☐ see lives changed/people get saved

☐ not let my teammates/family down

☐ produce big results to report after the trip, especially since many are supporting me

☐ be a great leader who knows just what to do and how to do it

☐ be a great teammate who doesn't complain or cause any trouble

I am EXCITED about

☐ going to a new place, meeting new people

☐ having new experiences in a new culture

☐ experiencing my first _____

☐ seeing God work in special ways in my life

☐ seeing God change people/bring them to faith

☐ going with a group and making new friends

☐ going with my family and bonding together

I feel Hopeful that

☐ this will be "the experience of a lifetime"

☐ I'll be changed; things will never be the same

☐ God will do amazing things

☐ I won't be as sinful as I normally am

☐ our team can make a real difference

☐ God will be glorified through me

I am EXPECTING to

☐ really help others and be used by God

☐ see my spiritual life deepen

☐ experience renewed intimacy with God

☐ see God work in ways I often overlook

☐ be part of God's kingdom in a different way

1. As you prepare to leave, what are your biggest fears?

....

....

....

....

....

....

2. Is there anything about the trip that makes you uneasy in the pit of your stomach when you think about it?

....

....

....

....

....

....

3. In what ways are you feeling needy?

....

....

....

....

....

4. What are your hopes and expectations for this trip?

....

....

....

....

....

....

5. What are you excited about seeing God do in you and through you?

....

....

....

....

....

....

PART 2: TALKING WITH GOD

Using the inventory and answers to the questions above, write a letter/prayer to God. Tell him about your needs and fears, your hopes and expectations as you head into this trip. As you write, consider:

- What do you want to see God do in you on this trip?
- Where are you feeling like you will have a hard time trusting God?
- What would you like to see God do through you on this trip?

PART 3: EMAILING YOUR SUPPORT TEAM

Nothing is more critical than to have a group of friends, family, and supporters who will pray for you daily while you are away. Using some of the concerns you've identified and some of the things you'd like to see God do on the trip, write them one short, final email, letting them know how they can pray.

GUIDELINES

1. **Be honest.** People will pray for you if they sense you are needy. So let them know what your needs really are, not just the surface issues. Use the work you did in Parts 1 and 2 to guide you about what to include.
2. **Be short.** You want people to be able to read your email quickly and pray specifically. A few sentences followed by a list of four to seven things is great.
3. **Be thankful.** Every single person on your list is someone special to you, someone who cares about you and who is going to pray for you. Let these people know how thankful you are for them.

TRAVELOGUE FEATURES

God has brought together just the right people at just the right time to accomplish the very things he wants to see done on your trip! Take a few minutes before you go, or early on, to record everyone who is on your team. Be sure to include any key on-site leaders where you will be serving (i.e., nationals, missionaries, people who run the long-term ministry on site, etc.).

Over the course of the trip, look for qualities or experiences that make you grateful for each person. During your time together, if you have the patience to look, you'll find out you're serving alongside some pretty amazing people!

Don't forget to get contact information so that you can easily stay in contact once you return.

MY TEAMMATES

Name	Why I'm Grateful for This Person	Contact Info

Name	Why I'm Grateful for This Person	Contact Info

Name	Why I'm Grateful for This Person	Contact Info

HOLDING THE ROPES

When rock climbing, you usually have someone standing at the bottom, called a belayer, who holds the ropes for you so you don't fall. Who are those back home who are "holding the ropes" for you during your trip? Who are those on your team of prayer and financial supporters? As you list their names here, you'll be amazed both now and in the future at how God faithfully provided a multitude of supporters to come alongside you and send you out. Use this list to follow up with your home team after your trip.

Name	Contact Info

Name	Contact Info

ON THE TRIP

I distinctly remember preparing for the first mission trip I ever took. I was in high school. A friend and I had signed up to spend an entire summer overseas doing outreach. As a new Christian, I was absolutely certain that this trip would be the secret ingredient that lit my spiritual life on fire. I assumed that my devotional life would blossom and I'd overcome all of those pesky "signature sins" that seemed to characterize my everyday life. No more doubts, no more struggles, no more setbacks. Just the "new and improved Patric," going to tell the rest of the world that they needed Jesus—big time. Imagine my surprise when I discovered that all of the same sins, doubts, and struggles had followed me to the field. In many ways, they seemed worse than ever!

That summer was one of the most spiritually formative events in my life, but in none of the ways I thought it would be. The lessons I began to learn that summer have taken many years to mature and bear fruit. But the enduring memory of that summer is that this was when I started to understand that my sin was a lot more deeply ingrained than I had ever imagined and, at the very same time, I was more loved by God than I ever dared to hope, all because of Jesus.

For the next ten days we're going to spend some time looking at scenes from the book of Acts. Each one will present us with the unique ways that the Holy Spirit works to motivate, sustain, and equip us for life-changing mission.

DAY 1

THE HOLY SPIRIT EQUIPS US TO JOIN GOD'S MISSION

BY PATRIC KNAAK

Patric Knaak serves as Serge's Deputy Director of Mission. He is the author of *On Mission: Devotions for Your Short-Term Trip* and coauthor of *Psalms: Real Prayers for Real Life*.

Date: ....

Location: ....

How I'll Be Serving Today: ....

....

....

BIG IDEA

Jesus has entrusted us with his mission to bring the gospel to the ends of the earth.

MEETING WITH GOD *(15 Minutes)*

JESUS TAKEN UP INTO HEAVEN (ACTS 1:4–14)

⁴On one occasion, while he was eating with them, he gave them this command: "Do not leave Jerusalem, but wait for the gift my Father promised, which you have heard me speak about. ⁵For John baptized with water, but in a few days you will be baptized with the Holy Spirit."

⁶Then they gathered around him and asked him, "Lord, are you at this time going to restore the kingdom to Israel?"

⁷He said to them: "It is not for you to know the times or dates the Father has set by his own authority. ⁸But you will receive power when the Holy Spirit comes on you; and you will be my witnesses in Jerusalem, and in all Judea and Samaria, and to the ends of the earth."

⁹After he said this, he was taken up before their very eyes, and a cloud hid him from their sight.

¹⁰They were looking intently up into the sky as he was going, when suddenly two men dressed in white stood beside them. ¹¹"Men of Galilee," they said, "why do you stand here looking into the sky? This same Jesus, who has been taken from you into heaven, will come back in the same way you have seen him go into heaven."

¹²Then the apostles returned to Jerusalem from the hill called the Mount of Olives, a Sabbath day's walk from the city. ¹³When they arrived, they went upstairs to the room where they were staying. Those present were Peter, John, James and Andrew; Philip and Thomas, Bartholomew and Matthew; James son of Alphaeus and Simon the Zealot, and Judas son of James. ¹⁴They all joined together constantly in prayer, along with the women and Mary the mother of Jesus, and with his brothers.

SURELY YOU'VE GOT A BETTER PLAN THAN THIS, RIGHT?

If you were a disciple, what would you have expected to happen after Jesus rose from the grave? Imagine that you had given up everything to follow Jesus for the last three years. During that time you had seen people flock to him to be healed and respond to his offer of salvation. And you too had experienced the power of the Holy Spirit to heal others in his name as you placed your trust in him for eternal life

(John 6:66–69). You had seen the terrifying opposition of the religious leaders steadily increase as they plotted against Jesus and had watched in horror as they made a mockery of justice, handing him over to the hated Roman occupiers for a brutal, humiliating execution. If you had experienced all of this, what would you expect to happen after Christ had risen from the dead? What would you think his next move should be, now that he had conquered death and had proven beyond a shadow of a doubt that he was the Messiah?

At least some part of my heart would want Jesus to display his full majesty, power, and glory right then and there to those that opposed him. The cruel religious leaders should be overturned, and the despised Roman oppressors vanquished. Mercy and justice would then flow down as Christ ruled here on earth. After all, no one could withstand the power of someone who had willingly laid down his life and then took it up again, rising from the dead. We get a hint that the disciples are also thinking along these lines when they ask, "Lord, are you at this time going to restore the kingdom to Israel?" (v. 6). It's a reasonable question. After all that they had been through, they want to know if now was the time when King Jesus would take over and bring about everything that God had promised to his people.

In response to their question, Jesus reminds us that God's kingdom rarely works the way we think it will. Instead of a rousing "Now *is* the time. Let's get to work and make all things new!" Jesus offers a gentle rebuke and a stunning set of instructions. He reminds his followers that the specifics of God's kingdom are under the sole discretion and authority of God the Father (v. 7). He goes on to tell them to keep waiting for the promised gift of the Holy Spirit. He knows that the Spirit would enable this small, ragged band of followers to carry out Jesus's audacious plan to bring about his kingdom (v. 8a). Through them, Jesus is going to spread the life-changing message of the gospel first locally in Jerusalem, then regionally in Judea and Samaria, and ultimately globally even to the ends of the earth (v. 8b). And then Jesus leaves. He ascends into heaven, leaving his followers staring into the sky (v. 9). Whatever the disciples had been anticipating, I don't think

Jesus leaving without first establishing his physical kingdom on earth was on anyone's radar.

Instead, God does what he has always done—he uses broken people to accomplish his purposes through the power of the Holy Spirit. Frankly, it's not what my human wisdom would have chosen. After all, wouldn't some angel armies and Christ triumphant have been a better way to ensure the spread of God's kingdom? At the very least, shouldn't Jesus have stayed on earth to be physically present and direct our efforts?

Yet God chooses to work through weak and needy people to spread the message of the gospel. Jesus doesn't offer any backups or alternatives. Having won salvation for his people, he entrusts the disciples to be his witnesses throughout the entire known world to bring his life-changing message to all people.

In fact, his plan hasn't changed in two thousand years. God *still* uses weak and needy people to accomplish his purposes. I don't always believe that though. Once on a mission trip, I was asked to be a driver to help get the team where we needed to go. The catch? The country used right-hand drive cars and drove on the left side of the road—the exact opposite of everything I was used to! I really wanted to be helpful. But I was also terrified of making a mistake, damaging the car, or putting my passengers in danger. In fact, in my heart I was resentful that I was being put in such a stressful position.

But that is exactly where God most wants to meet us. Throughout the course of the week, every time we needed to go up a tight mountain road or drive through the exceedingly narrow lanes in the village, I was desperately praying that Jesus would show up and help me. Part of the paradoxical nature of God's kingdom is that it grows *inside* of us as we learn to trust him, while it grows *outside* of us as we step out in faith to love and serve others. Jesus wanted more from me than simply getting the team from point A to point B. He also wanted to use my anxiety and fear to show me just how deeply I needed him and how capable he was of meeting my needs.

There are no superheroes in the missionary world. The missionaries you will serve alongside, as well as you and your team, are no different than the disciples on that day when they stood looking up at the clouds wondering where Jesus had just gone. Like the disciples, we don't always understand what God is up to. And we know that our own strength is never equal to the task at hand. But God's is.

So as you start your trip, begin looking for those places where you are utterly dependent on the Holy Spirit to get you through the day. Learn to let those places of fear, grumbling, or frustration serve as divine reminders to turn and run back to Christ. He doesn't need you to be perfect. He invites you to be dependent on him. Why? That's the place where he has the greatest freedom to work through you. And as he does, we too receive the type of power that only the Holy Spirit can provide.

RESPONDING TO GOD *(15 Minutes)*

Use these questions for personal reflection.

1. Just like the disciples in our passage today, everyone has their own internal expectations about what they want to see God do. As you start your trip, it's helpful to name them so that throughout the trip you are able to bring them before the Lord and surrender them to him.

    - What expectations do you have for yourself on this trip?
    - What expectations do you have for others on this trip?
    - What expectations do you have for what God will do on this trip?

    ....

    ....

    ....

    ....

    ....

2. Jesus tells his disciples that they will be losing his physical presence but gaining the presence and the power of the Holy Spirit instead.

   - How comfortable are you with relying on the Holy Spirit in your daily life?
   - Where would you like to see him work more deeply in you and through you on this trip?

   ....

   ....

   ....

   ....

   ....

3. The Holy Spirit works both inwardly and outwardly in our lives at the same time. The chart below helps explain how our inward experience and outward actions are fueled by God's grace. Take a few minutes to review the chart then answer the questions below.

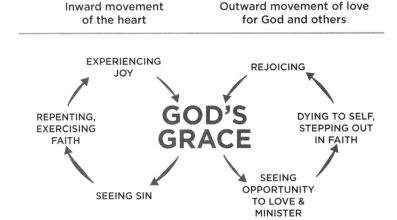

Inward movement of the heart	Outward movement of love for God and others

EXPERIENCING JOY

REJOICING

REPENTING, EXERCISING FAITH

GOD'S GRACE

DYING TO SELF, STEPPING OUT IN FAITH

SEEING SIN

SEEING OPPORTUNITY TO LOVE & MINISTER

   - It may seem counterintuitive that seeing our sin is connected to seeing opportunity to love and minister. But if we do not see our sin more clearly, including those sins that stay primarily in our thoughts and hearts, we'll never be free to love others. Where have you seen some of your own sin more clearly since you've been on the trip?

....

....

....

....

....

- Repenting of our sin—even if no one else knows about it— requires the Holy Spirit to work in our hearts. And when we repent, we receive God's forgiveness, his assurance that we are his children, and his love through the power of the Holy Spirit as well. Why do you think this internal repentance and faith is so essential if we are also going to die to self externally by stepping out in faith to love and serve others? Spend some time praying that the Holy Spirit will do just that during the rest of your trip.

....

....

....

....

....

WHAT I SAW GOD DO TODAY

This evening (or tomorrow morning), take a few minutes to record unique ways that you saw God at work. Our sin-hardened hearts easily forget, so writing down a few of the things you've seen God do is a great way to offer thanks and praise to him.

Today I saw God . . .

....

....

....

....

....

THE HOLY SPIRIT'S POWER SUSTAINS US ON MISSION

BY JEREMY SINK

Jeremy Sink has served as a missionary and church planter in Japan since 2012. He and his wife Gina joined Serge in 2018 and now serve as team leaders for the team in Nagoya.

Date: ....

Location: ....

How I'll Be Serving Today: ....

....

....

BIG IDEA

The Holy Spirit empowers us for Jesus's mission.

MEETING WITH GOD *(15 Minutes)*

THE HOLY SPIRIT COMES AT PENTECOST (ACTS 2:1–6, 37–41)

[1] When the day of Pentecost came, they were all together in one place. [2] Suddenly a sound like the blowing of a violent wind came from heaven and filled the whole house where they were sitting. [3] They saw what seemed to be tongues of fire that separated and came to rest on each of them. [4] All of them were filled with the Holy Spirit and began to speak in other tongues as the Spirit enabled them.

[5] Now there were staying in Jerusalem God-fearing Jews from every nation under heaven. [6] When they heard this sound, a crowd came together in bewilderment, because each one heard their own language being spoken.

* * *

[37] When the people heard this, they were cut to the heart and said to Peter and the other apostles, "Brothers, what shall we do?"

[38] Peter replied, "Repent and be baptized, every one of you, in the name of Jesus Christ for the forgiveness of your sins. And you will receive the gift of the Holy Spirit. [39] The promise is for you and your children and for all who are far off—for all whom the Lord our God will call."

[40] With many other words he warned them; and he pleaded with them, "Save yourselves from this corrupt generation." [41] Those who accepted his message were baptized, and about three thousand were added to their number that day.

ARE YOU WEAK ENOUGH TO SEE GOD WORK?

On my first short-term trip to Japan, I had the opportunity to lead a Bible study with a group of Japanese women. It was on that familiar passage where Jesus cast demons out of the young man in Luke 8. My talk revolved around how the man on the other side of the lake wasn't asking for help. Jesus showed up uninvited to deliver him from a problem he didn't even want help with. As I closed, one of the women became very emotional. She said, "I wish I could believe in that kind of God; that story sounds almost too good to be true!"

In the same way as Jesus in that story, the Holy Spirit moves toward us in unexpected and even uninvited ways. Cross-cultural missions is like a laboratory for unmasking weaknesses and exposing our sinful hearts. How can we make a difference in a place where we can't speak the language and don't understand the nuances of the culture? How do we share the good news of Jesus with people who don't know what sin is and have never even heard that there is a personal God who lovingly made the heavens and the earth? And on a one- to two-week trip, maybe the most pressing question is how do we do *anything* in the midst of jet lag and exhaustion? Could it be that God plans to use your areas of greatest personal weakness to work in and through you during this trip—even in ways that are uninvited?

Acts 2 represents a major new development in the history of God's redemptive work. Around thirty years earlier, the long-promised Messiah had come. Jesus lived the life we couldn't live, died the death we deserved, and rose from the grave in a display of victory over sin and death. He sent his disciples out into the world to share the good news. It was an impossibly big task, but it came with an equally great promise: "And surely I am with you always, to the very end of the age" (Matthew 28:20).

In the first verses of this chapter in Acts, the Spirit's coming is described with words that show his power. The sound of a mighty rushing wind fills the room (v. 2). Tongues of fire rest on those who are gathered (v. 3). Those are frightening images, but this is not a display of power designed to chase people away. Instead, God is beginning to gather his people, scattered among all the nations of the world, into his family. Nothing is more comforting than hearing your own language spoken in a foreign land. The diverse people staying in Jerusalem hear sounds of home coming out of the mouths of these disciples as they proclaim the gospel in each person's native language (v. 6)!

And then Peter stands up to tell the crowd about their true home. He tells the story that we continue to carry to the nations today. It's the story of the Father's love, the Son's sacrifice, and the Spirit's coming. Perhaps the greatest display of the Spirit's power on the day of Pentecost is his unlikely choice in using Peter—Peter who had so recently denied Jesus on the night before his crucifixion—to deliver that good news. Our God loves to use weak and broken people who have experienced his mercy as his ambassadors. All glory be to God—none to us!

As Peter speaks, the Holy Spirit presses the gospel message home. Short- and long-term missionaries often need interpreters in order to communicate with native speakers of the local language. As we carry the gospel, we always need a kind of heart-translation that only the Spirit can give, because he is the one who takes the message of the gospel and makes it powerful. He is the one who opens blind eyes and replaces hearts of stone with hearts that love God. The people in the crowd "were cut to the heart" and cried out, "What shall we do?" (v. 37). By the end of the day, three thousand turned to Jesus (v. 41).

Every day, short-term mission trips let us experience God working in and through our weaknesses as we learn to trust the power and presence of the Holy Spirit to accomplish his purposes. At home we often default to hanging out with people who act and think the same way we do. We choose activities that demonstrate our competence and avoid places that feel risky or that might expose our weaknesses. On a short-term trip, all of that is stripped away. We are often challenged to step into situations in which we aren't very skilled and face needs that feel overwhelming. As we do, we also get the opportunity to repent of trusting ourselves and instead have to rely deeply on God. Maybe you didn't know you were signing up for that! As uncomfortable as that may feel, it's also a precious opportunity to lean into the presence and power of the Spirit today.

As you serve others today, the promise of the gift of the Holy Spirit is "for you and your children" (v. 39). And it's for the people around you today "whom the Lord our God will call" to himself (v. 39). The gospel "is the power of God that brings salvation to everyone who believes" (Romans 1:16). So as you take the good news of Jesus to others, spend some time receiving it for yourself. Remember that the same things that were true for the disciples at Pentecost are still true for you today: God's power isn't limited by your weakness. The Holy Spirit has come. You are not alone. He is with you. He will empower you to do all that he commands. He is the one who produces fruit—not us, not our gifts and abilities. You are loved. You are secure. You are free to lay down your life to love others. Those are gifts worth having, even if we need to let go of our own agendas and abilities.

RESPONDING TO GOD *(15 Minutes)*

Learning to listen to God and depend on his Holy Spirit to work through us takes some intentionality on our part, especially when we are stepping into new situations. The following five-minute drill is a way to learn how to do this. It's something you can do anytime, anywhere. Work through the following explanation and exercise now, and then look for ways to use it today and throughout the rest of the trip.

NOTICE WHEN YOU'RE FEELING OUT OF SORTS
(1 minute)

Pay attention to any time you feel overwhelmed, out of control, anxious, frustrated, scared, like you are all alone, etc. These are usually signs that something isn't right in your heart and that God would like to talk with you about something.

In the last day or two, where have you felt "out of sorts" emotionally or spiritually?

> *Example:* I just got assigned to the door-to-door evangelism team for the day and I'm feeling a lot of anxiety about it.

....

....

....

....

....

ASK THE HOLY SPIRIT TO REVEAL YOUR UNBELIEF
(1 minute)

Even if you are keeping calm on the surface, whenever you notice that you're feeling unsettled, spend a minute or two asking the Holy Spirit to reveal what is going on in your heart. Often it's caused by our unbelief—there is something about the gospel or about Christ that we are not receiving, trusting, or relying on. Or it may be caused by something we are holding onto too tightly like looking good in front of others, or needing to be in control.

Holy Spirit, where am I not believing something about God, his love for me, or his provision for me?

> *Example*: I think the reason I am so anxious is that I am afraid I will look foolish, or that the people who answer the door will immediately reject me. I don't like being in situations where I'm not in control and I'm feeling like God has left me all alone in this.

....

....

....

....

....

LISTEN FOR THE HOLY SPIRIT TO REMIND YOU OF THE GOSPEL *(2 minutes)*

Once the Holy Spirit has helped you identify where you may not be believing the gospel, ask him to help you see how God is able to meet your needs. Scripture, the words of a worship song, and spending time recounting God's promises or past answers to prayer are all great ways to be reminded of the truth of the gospel.

Holy Spirit, now that I'm starting to see what I'm not believing about God, remind me what is true, based on God's Word.

> *Example:* In light of my anxiety, I need to cling to God's promises.
>
> - I'm not alone; God is always with me and he's always in control (Isaiah 41:10).
> - God's power is perfected in my weakness (2 Corinthians 12:9).
> - I'm here to love others because Jesus has first loved me (1 John 4:9–12).
> - It's okay if I look foolish because my reputation is established by Christ's work on the cross, not by what I do or fail to do (Philippians 3:8–9).

....

....

....

....

....

REENGAGE THE SITUATION *(1 minute)*

Now that you've had a little gospel perspective restored, it's time to reengage the situation. Remember that no matter what the task is, God is right there with you. He wants to partner with you to accomplish his work. He's the "senior partner" and you're the "junior partner," so you can always look to him for his leading when you aren't sure what to do.

How does God want to partner with me in order to see my trust and dependence on him grow, as we do the work at hand?

> *Example:* Okay, I'm going to knock on a door and when I do, I'm going to trust that my Father is in charge, that he loves the people who live there (even if I'm scared of them!), and that he wants to work in and through my fear to connect with them.

....

....

....

....

....

This process is a helpful way to be sensitive throughout the day, encouraging us to be continually aware of and dependent on the Holy Spirit. It's more about changing your mindset than about adding more tasks to your list. And because it's not about "measuring up spiritually" but rather about being more aware of the needs we already have, it allows our needs to drive us back to Christ. We'll check back in on this process later in the week to see how things are going.

WHAT I SAW GOD DO TODAY

This evening (or tomorrow morning), take a few minutes to record unique ways that you saw God at work. Our sin-hardened hearts easily forget, so writing down a few of the things you've seen God do is a great way to offer thanks and praise to him.

Today I saw God . . .

....

....

....

....

....

THE HOLY SPIRIT REMINDS US EVERYONE NEEDS THE GOSPEL

BY EMILY SHRADER

Emily Shrader and her family served with Serge overseas for more than a decade. She is now a Renewal Specialist for Serge and resides in North Carolina, where her husband David serves as a chaplain in the United States Air Force.

Date: ....

Location: ....

How I'll Be Serving Today:..

....

....

BIG IDEA

Salvation comes by grace alone, through faith alone in Christ. There is no other name under heaven by which we must be saved.

MEETING WITH GOD *(15 Minutes)*

PETER HEALS A LAME BEGGAR AND TESTIFIES BEFORE THE SANHEDRIN (ACTS 3:1–10; 4:5–13)

[1] One day Peter and John were going up to the temple at the time of prayer—at three in the afternoon. [2] Now a man who was lame from birth was being carried to the temple gate called Beautiful, where he was put every day to beg from those going into the temple courts. [3] When he saw Peter and John about to enter, he asked them for money. [4] Peter looked straight at him, as did John. Then Peter said, "Look at us!" [5] So the man gave them his attention, expecting to get something from them.

[6] Then Peter said, "Silver or gold I do not have, but what I do have I give you. In the name of Jesus Christ of Nazareth, walk." [7] Taking him by the right hand, he helped him up, and instantly the man's feet and ankles became strong. [8] He jumped to his feet and began to walk. Then he went with them into the temple courts, walking and jumping, and praising God. [9] When all the people saw him walking and praising God, [10] they recognized him as the same man who used to sit begging at the temple gate called Beautiful, and they were filled with wonder and amazement at what had happened to him.

* * *

[5] The next day the rulers, the elders and the teachers of the law met in Jerusalem. [6] Annas the high priest was there, and so were Caiaphas, John, Alexander and others of the high priest's family. [7] They had Peter and John brought before them and began to question them: "By what power or what name did you do this?"

[8] Then Peter, filled with the Holy Spirit, said to them: "Rulers and elders of the people! [9] If we are being called to account today for an act of kindness shown to a man who was lame and are being asked how he was healed, [10] then know this, you and all the people of Israel: It is by the name of Jesus Christ of Nazareth, whom you crucified but whom God raised from the dead, that this man stands before you healed. [11] Jesus is

"'the stone you builders rejected,
    which has become the cornerstone.'

¹²Salvation is found in no one else, for there is no other name under heaven given to mankind by which we must be saved."

¹³When they saw the courage of Peter and John and realized that they were unschooled, ordinary men, they were astonished and they took note that these men had been with Jesus.

EXCEEDING EXPECTATIONS

What do you suppose the lame man thought as he woke up on the morning of his healing? What were his expectations for the day? We know he planned to be laid at the Beautiful Gate since his friends carried him there daily (v. 2). He expected to be given money (vv. 3, 5), so we also know that he was relying on the goodwill and generosity of others in order to get what he needed to survive. And we can assume that he had been doing this for a long time since he was "lame from birth" (v. 2). I imagine this man expected this day to be like every other day.

How about Peter and John? What might have been their expectations for the day when they rose from their mats and said their morning prayers? Unlike the man who spent every day of his life begging, their recent experiences had been anything but routine. These two fishermen had been called by Jesus and had followed him through much of his earthly ministry. They had been part of his inner circle, had listened to his teachings, and had seen him perform many miracles. They had been present for Jesus's death and resurrection and had witnessed him ascend into heaven. Now they had received the Holy Spirit, and Peter himself delivered a sermon that led to three thousand people giving their lives to Christ! I imagine Peter and John, apostles of Jesus Christ, expected this day to be anything but ordinary.

Though we can only imagine what these men were thinking and hoping at the start of the day, we can be certain of what actually happened, thanks to this wonderful account of an extraordinary encounter. This lame man expected money, and Peter and John, having no silver or gold, healed him in the name of Jesus instead (v. 6).

Like the lame man, the world around you is burdened with neediness. People feel their need and think they know what will give them relief. It's our privilege to meet them in their need and offer them even more than they could ask or imagine—the hope of Jesus Christ. Their truest, deepest needs are met by grace alone, through faith alone in Christ. We believe, as Peter declares, "there is no other name under heaven . . . by which we must be saved" (v. 12).

Once, while living in North Africa, I found myself in conversation with a young man I'd just met—we were both waiting on friends who were negotiating a rental agreement. He began to talk about how he thought Islam and Christianity were basically the same thing. In my heart I rolled my eyes; I was hesitant to "get into it" with this guy. I just wanted my friends to decide if they were going to rent the house and then get back to my day. I sighed and answered dutifully, "Actually, they're really not the same thing. Christians believe something very different than Muslims." He then surprised me by asking, "What do you believe?"

I never expected such an open, honest question. I was used to people insisting they already knew what I believed. So I took a moment, prayed, and said, "Do you really want to know what I believe? Because it's going to blow your mind." I proceeded to share the gospel with him. He listened, wide-eyed, as I told him that I believed Jesus died for the forgiveness of my sins and that . . . wait for it . . . three days later God raised him from the dead! I encouraged him to read more about the life, death, and resurrection of Jesus in the *Injil* (the Arabic word for the Gospels). As our friends joined us on the porch and our conversation ended, I watched him walk out the front gate and wondered if he'd actually read more about Jesus. I prayed that he would.

In hindsight, I wish I would have been more expectant for how God might use me that day. Even so, I'm thankful that in spite of my hesitancy, apathy, and cynicism—all borne out of self-reliance and my own struggle with unbelief—Jesus still made himself known to that young man.

Evangelism comes naturally to some, but for most of us it can be intimidating. Idols of our hearts—like approval, comfort, and security—can form barriers to stepping out in faith and sharing about Jesus. Even our own doubts about God can keep us from proclaiming the gospel. When I'm confronted with my fear of man or my lack of passion to talk about Jesus with others, it's easy to begin to despair and even feel guilty. But that isn't what Jesus wants from us. He offers us a different, better way in which our need for him becomes part of the very story we share with others. Jesus invites us to bring our heart idols to him in repentance, and he gladly breaks them to pieces and assures us that he is with us. As his Spirit reorients us, he empowers us to keep telling others about him with renewed faith and fresh gratitude for the gospel at work in our own lives.

The result is a freedom and boldness that will get people's attention. Let's consider the people who witness the healing of the lame man. What were their expectations for the day? We can assume their expectations were a lot like those of the beggar—nothing special, just another day. But when they saw the man walking and recognize him as the lame one they had seen lying on a mat with outstretched hands day after day after day, they were "filled with wonder and amazement" (3:10)! And when the priests and scribes asked Peter and John by what authority they have healed the man, they responded with a definitive answer: "know this, you and all the people of Israel: It is by the name of Jesus Christ of Nazareth, whom you crucified but whom God raised from the dead, that this man stands before you healed" (4:10). The priests and scribes were astonished at their boldness. And then it says, "they took note that these men had been with Jesus"(4:13).

As you think ahead about your day, what expectations do you have? It's possible you will encounter all sorts of people with all sorts of needs. You may have the opportunity to participate in the restorative work of God's kingdom by giving something tangible—medical care for the under-resourced, your strength to a building project, or your time to a kids' camp. But all of the people you meet—like Peter and John, like the beggar and the teachers of the law in today's passage—need the hope that the gospel brings.

RESPONDING TO GOD *(15 Minutes)*

1. As Christians, we continue to need the same gospel message that
    the audience at Pentecost and the rulers in Jerusalem needed—that
    Jesus alone saves us and makes us right with God, totally apart from
    our efforts. However, it's easy to turn to other things, people, or our
    own abilities to bring us rest, relief, comfort, protection, joy—in
    short, to "save" us.

    - What is an area on this trip in which you feel fear, vulnerability,
      discomfort, or weakness?
    - What are you turning to, other than the gospel, to "save" you in
      this area? In other words, what are you depending on besides
      Jesus to free you from those negative emotions?
    - How does your need for the same gospel—for your salvation
      and your continued life as a follower of Jesus—help you bet-
      ter love, serve, and proclaim the gospel to the people you're
      serving?

    ....

    ....

    ....

    ....

    ....

2. Ask the Holy Spirit to bring to mind a specific person you've met
    on this trip that he'd like you to share the gospel with. If you haven't
    met someone yet who fits into that category, think of someone back
    home who needs to hear the good news about Jesus.

    - What hesitations or fears do you have about sharing with this
      person?
    - What truths of the gospel do you need to remember for yourself
      to help you share with him or her with freedom and boldness?

- Spend a few minutes asking God to provide you with an opportunity to share with this person, to give you compassion and boldness when you do share, and for the Holy Spirit to be working in both of your hearts before and during your conversation.

....

....

....

....

....

WHAT I SAW GOD DO TODAY

This evening (or tomorrow morning), take a few minutes to record unique ways that you saw God at work. Our sin-hardened hearts easily forget, so writing down a few of the things you've seen God do is a great way to offer thanks and praise to him.

Today I saw God . . .

....

....

....

....

....

DAY 4

THE HOLY SPIRIT CREATES SACRIFICIAL UNITY IN US

BY MARC DAVIS

Marc Davis joined Serge's Renewal Team in 2019 as the Program Leader for Global Learning and now serves as the Associate Director of Renewal. He is the author of *Job: Where Is God in My Suffering?* and a frequent guest speaker for churches and Serge events.

Date: ....

Location: ....

How I'll Be Serving Today: ....

....

....

BIG IDEA

Because we are all one in Christ, we are to have all things in common, particularly as we serve on mission.

MEETING WITH GOD *(15 Minutes)*
THE BELIEVERS SHARE THEIR POSSESSIONS (ACTS 4:32–35)

[32] All the believers were one in heart and mind. No one claimed that any of their possessions was their own, but they shared everything they had. [33] With great power the apostles continued to testify to the resurrection of the Lord Jesus. And God's grace was so powerfully at work in them all [34] that there were no needy persons among them. For from time to time those who owned land or houses sold them, brought the money from the sales [35] and put it at the apostles' feet, and it was distributed to anyone who had need. [36] Joseph, a Levite from Cyprus, whom the apostles called Barnabas (which means "son of encouragement"), [37] sold a field he owned and brought the money and put it at the apostles' feet.

I WANT WHAT I WANT

My friends and I were received warmly when we arrived at a Christian hospital serving low-income patients in South Asia. Our accommodations were simple but comfortable, and all of our needs were taken care of. There were some things to get used to, of course: there was no warm running water, so every morning we took turns using an immersion heater to warm up water in a bucket so that we could wash. And though the food was plentiful, we had to be very careful about what we ate; my stomach was often at least a little out of sorts during our visit, and sometimes worse.

But of course that was all part of the adventure and would make our stories better when we got home! Still, what was an adventure on day one was a trial by day three, and it became harder each day to be entirely content and happy.

As the days went by, my desires became sharper, particularly *I want a hot shower* and *I want a settled, happy stomach!* It became harder to lay down my sense of entitlement, to be content to hold loosely the things that I wanted.

Wherever we are, part of the challenge of the Christian life is the need to wrangle with our desires. *I want what I want* is a very strong instinct, as is also its close cousin, *This is mine and I don't want to give it up!* Those instincts are with us always, everywhere, and exist in competition with the desire to know Jesus and find life in him. But they can come to the surface even more when we're away from home and deprived of some of the creature comforts to which we're accustomed.

These verses in Acts 4 describe a remarkable season in the life of the early church. Two things are going on at once, and the one has to do with the other.

First, we read in verse 33 that "with great power the apostles continued to testify to the resurrection of the Lord Jesus." The message of the gospel is being articulated for all to hear: Jesus is alive! As in the sermons recorded in the first chapters of Acts, that proclamation of the resurrection is shorthand for much more: *Jesus is the Messiah. God has brought salvation through him. Everyone who believes in him will receive forgiveness of sins and the gift of the Spirit.* As the apostles proclaim the message, the Holy Spirit makes their words powerful and effective, and many men and women believe.

While the message of the gospel is being powerfully proclaimed to those *outside* the church, the gospel is also powerfully at work *inside* the church, shaping them into a new kind of Christian community. Luke tells us that "God's grace was . . . powerfully at work in them all" (v. 33). Grace is not just the entranceway into the community; it is an ongoing, living expression of the presence of God in and among them all. The new believers have not just joined a club; they become swept up in a **movement of grace.** God in the person of the Holy Spirit is living among them and transforming their community life.

That movement of grace in Acts 4 took on a particular, remarkable expression. The community of faith was characterized by an obvious unity; it was amazingly, noticeably free of factions, envy, or party spirit. But there was also this specific way of relating to one another that quickly became part of their shared culture: "No one claimed that any of their possessions was their own, but they shared everything they had" (v. 32). The gospel loosened their grasp on the things that they owned, even to the degree that many would have said, "Nothing that is 'mine' is mine to keep; all of it is available to the Lord for the needs of the community." And in that spirit, as needs arose, those who had a little more would from time to time liquidate a possession to free up funds to meet the needs of others. It was amazing—and certainly would've gotten the attention of outsiders who had contact with the church.

As you walk through this week together with your team, you may be experiencing your trip on more than one level. On the one hand, you're seeing an amazing new place, meeting people, participating with the local Christian community, and hearing (and maybe proclaiming) the gospel. There are exciting things to see and hear and be a part of. And maybe, away from home, this gospel is sounding richer, truer—and its effects are being displayed with a different kind of power.

But at the same time, you may be doing physical work you're not accustomed to. The food might not be great. The bugs might be eating you alive. Maybe you're sick, or somebody in the bed next to you snores, or somebody's not pulling their weight in the work. There are things you want that you can't have. And maybe what you do have—a better bed or an easier work assignment or a secret stash of snacks—you're inclined to clutch a little tighter to yourself. You may have already had a conflict with a teammate over these things, or maybe it's simmering just below the surface.

How does the proclamation of the gospel, which you are participating in, intersect with "your desires that battle within you" (James 4:1)? The movement of God's grace in the early Jerusalem church caused a powerful proclamation of the gospel and also a revolution in the hearts of the believers. In the midst of the kingdom movement that you are a part of this week, know this: *Jesus isn't just in pursuit of people who don't know him. He's after you, too! He wants your heart.* He invites you to loosen your grip on what you want, on your sense of the way things should go for the rest of the week. As Barnabas sold the field that belonged to him by right, so also take what's yours and bring it to Jesus's feet—your comfort, your security, your desire for _____ (fill in the blank!)—and give it over to him. Make that space in your heart available to him for him to possess. It is, after all, his already.

As we talk to Jesus about our desires, as we relinquish our hold on what is (or what we think ought to be) ours, we are making space for the gospel to move with power among us and also through us.

RESPONDING TO GOD *(15 Minutes)*

1. Where have you been struggling with "I-want-what-I-want syn-drome" on the trip so far? If you can't immediately think of something, where have you been grumbling or complaining, even if it's just to yourself?

....

....

....

....

2. In the passage, Barnabas sold the field that belonged to him and gave the profit to the apostles to use to meet others' needs.

    • Where do you sense Jesus is inviting you to release something and lay it at his feet for the sake of others? It could be related to your comfort, your control, or your sense of security. Or maybe it's something else that you have a hard time surrendering to him.

    ....

    ....

    ....

    ....

3. Giving up things we want for the sake of loving others and maintaining unity is really hard. But God doesn't just ask us to give up things. He offers us much better things that will actually satisfy us more.

- Now that you've considered some of your wants that you may need to surrender to him on the trip, what is he offering you that is better?

Example: "It's really hard for me to share accommodations because I'm a light sleeper and everyone else disturbs me during the night. In fact, I'm getting a bit resentful about it. But there are things I need even more than a good night's sleep, like spending intimate time talking with Jesus and listening to him. When I'm lying awake at night, I can pour out my heart to him. I can ask him to help me see what he accomplished through our team today. I can confess how much I'm struggling. Those are things I usually don't have time to do during the day. So the times when I can't sleep are sort of 'bonus times' with Jesus."

....

....

....

....

....

WHAT I SAW GOD DO TODAY

This evening (or tomorrow morning), take a few minutes to record unique ways that you saw God at work. Our sin-hardened hearts easily forget, so writing down a few of the things you've seen God do is a great way to offer thanks and praise to him.

Today I saw God . . .

....

....

....

....

....

DAY

THE HOLY SPIRIT WALKS WITH US THROUGH SUFFERING

BY JENNIFER MYHRE

Dr. Jennifer Myhre has served with Serge in East Africa for three decades as a pediatrician, team leader, area director, writer, and mom. Jennifer is the author of the popular fiction series *The Rwendigo Tales*, featuring characters and themes inspired by her life in Africa.

Date: ....

Location: ....

How I'll Be Serving Today: ....

....

....

BIG IDEA

Jesus's path led through both suffering and glory, and so does ours as we follow him.

MEETING WITH GOD (15 Minutes)

THE STONING OF STEPHEN (ACTS 7:54-60)

[54] When the members of the Sanhedrin heard [Stephen's rebuke], they were furious and gnashed their teeth at him. [55] But Stephen, full of the Holy Spirit, looked up to heaven and saw the glory of God, and Jesus standing at the right hand of God. [56] "Look," he said, "I see heaven open and the Son of Man standing at the right hand of God."

[57] At this they covered their ears and, yelling at the top of their voices, they all rushed at him, [58] dragged him out of the city and began to stone him. Meanwhile, the witnesses laid their coats at the feet of a young man named Saul.

[59] While they were stoning him, Stephen prayed, "Lord Jesus, receive my spirit." [60] Then he fell on his knees and cried out, "Lord, do not hold this sin against them." When he had said this, he fell asleep.

STONES AND THRONES

What did you expect this mission trip to look like? Take a minute to remember your pre-trip imaginings of how you'd spend each day, and then jot a list of things you did yesterday in question 1 of the Responding to God section below. What strikes you about the difference?

In Acts 6, the church community had taken on the family responsibility to care for widows by distributing food, but some begin to suspect that their particular ethnolinguistic group had been unfairly slighted (v. 1). Complaint and dissension stirs the group, as so often happens with any mixture of humans! The disciples gather and decide to delegate this contentious job to seven new deacons, including Stephen (vv. 5–6).

Like Jesus, these first-generation leaders assume their job involved *both* caring for the bodily needs of new believers *and* grasping God's work of redemption that underpinned their actions. Stephen waits tables and also studies the arc of Hebrew history. He both plans for cooking and calories and seating capacity and thinks through the parallels between patriarchs and the purposes of God's presence with humans.

In 6:8–15 we see that both Stephen's actions and teaching disrupt the status quo. It doesn't take long for the good these deacons are doing to stir up the attention of those who feel their own control or prestige threatened. Paradoxically, doing good often stirs up evil.

Do you think Stephen expected the debate to turn violent? Once he got pushback, perhaps he considered hiding his opinions or dialing down his feeding program? We wonder sometimes if a negative result means we should change our course. Our family went to western Uganda thirty years ago as medical missionaries. We joined a small team serving among a very marginalized people with an unwritten language, no Bible, and the most dire statistics in the country for everything—which is saying a lot in a place recovering from the brutal dictator Idi Amin. In our fourth year, a rebel group crossed the nearby border and attacked our home, forcing us to scoop up our kids and flee for our lives on foot through the bush. Many of our neighbors were killed, and the entire area was thrown into disarray. As we recovered and processed, we asked if this was a clear message from God that our mission there was done. We'd just about finished the term of our initial commitment, so maybe it was time to change course, to leave permanently. Sometimes God does get our attention with hardship. But what if this was not a sign to quit or change, but a part of the "take up your cross" pattern that Jesus modeled? What if a dangerous and confusing turn of events could still be in God's plan?

Stephen could have gone into hiding when opposition kept building. Instead he stays in Jerusalem. With much input and prayer, we also returned to our Ugandan home after the first rebel attack—and again and again over the years, after being scraped along many more rough edges of this broken world, from hostile court cases to tropical illnesses to the loss of friends. Being on mission does not magically insulate us from suffering. Instead, it often seems to bring us directly into suffering's path.

As Stephen continues his work and his testimony, he finds himself in front of the Sanhedrin (6:12), a court of Jewish elders with both religious and legal jurisdiction. To explain himself, he reaches back to the common denominator of shared belief and shared story (7:2–47). Beginning with Abraham, he retells their history, emphasizing God's plan to redeem the whole world, not just one nation. He reminds them that their ancestral leaders habitually rejected individuals who had miraculously encountered God. He reminds them that God still pursued presence with them, in the tabernacle, in the temple, and in Jesus. When Stephen reaches the present (vv. 48–53), he quotes Isaiah 66 to explode their small view of God. God is the one whom all of heaven and earth cannot contain, let alone one temple. Free food for old women perhaps had been a threat to their popularity, but the leaders realize this exegesis threatens their power as the only arbiters of the divine. The legal hearing turns into a mob of angry men throwing stones (vv. 57–58).

Stephen certainly suffers hard work, menial labor, misunderstanding, opposition, and weariness. Most people on mission do. Now he suffers physical pain and death (v. 60). He becomes the first martyr.

The most striking thing about this story to me is that *at the very moment* that Stephen is being dragged to be stoned, he sees Jesus ruling at God's right hand (v. 55). Stones and thrones are not mutually incompatible.

This is one of the paradoxes our human hearts and brains struggle with most. Suffering does not come our way because Jesus is not able to help us. Jesus's resurrection victory remains true even though we do not yet experience the full extent of his saving rule. He is currently—right now—glorified, and that glory is seeping into our reality and transforming it, through people like Stephen and me and you. God allows us to see that glory at times as the hungry are fed, the sick are cured, the unreached believe, a water project is completed. God also allows us to suffer. Only God understands the mystery of that paradox.

In Stephen's death, we see these truths play out in all their complexity. He follows Jesus's example in practical, hands-on care of the poor, bringing some measure of justice and comfort by foreshadowing the new society Jesus came to create. He follows Christ's teaching, testifying faithfully to God's purpose to dwell among us in perfect love. And yet, none of that prevents him from suffering the full assault of evil; it actually seems to make him a lightning rod. He is questioned, ostracized, shamed, excluded, pushed, threatened, then hit repeatedly with stones. As that sorrow unfolds, God allows him to see truth: at the very moment when evil seems to be winning, Jesus shines in powerful glory in a dimension few get to see in daily life. Stephen realizes the end of the story is glory, not defeat. That allows him to feel concern for his accusers and ask for God to forgive them (v. 60). He does not ask for revenge; he asks for wholeness, for God's love to so permeate the world that stoning would no longer be an event or a concern.

We can't explain the moment-to-moment interplay of stones and thrones. But like Stephen, we can say, "Receive my spirit," as we lay our lives and all justice in the hands of Love.

RESPONDING TO GOD (15 Minutes)

1. What did you expect this trip to look like? What role did you antic- ipate playing?

....

....

....

....

....

Now list a few things you've spent most of your time on in the last few days.

....

....

....

....

....

How do the lists compare? What surprises you?

....

....

....

....

Finish reading the rest of the devotion before completing the following questions.

2.   Reflecting on your lists from question 1, does your work seem valuable? Do you feel invisible or honored? Are your gifts being appreciated or ignored?

....

....

....

....

Stephen didn't get earthly accolades or rewards for his faithful service to God, but because he could see the goodness and glory of Christ so clearly, he was willing to suffer and die in pursuit of his call. In what ways might God be calling you to serve him on this trip without the appreciation or fulfillment you expected?

....

....

....

....

3. As we follow Jesus on mission, we will experience suffering as we die to self. We may not have literal stones thrown at us. Instead, our suffering might look like conflict with others or doing tasks we don't like. When have you most struggled to see God's presence in your suffering?

....

....

....

....

....

4. Stephen, following Jesus's example, prayed for forgiveness for his persecutors as he was dying. How does Jesus's current glory give you the capacity to forgive others who might be adding to your difficulties?

....

....

....

....

....

Note: if you are struggling to forgive someone on your team, spend a few minutes throughout the day imagining Jesus on his throne while you and the person who makes you suffer are both sitting at his feet. What would you say to this person in front of Jesus?

WHAT I SAW GOD DO TODAY

This evening (or tomorrow morning), take a few minutes to record unique ways that you saw God at work. Our sin-hardened hearts easily forget, so writing down a few of the things you've seen God do is a great way to offer thanks and praise to him.

Today I saw God . . .

....

....

....

....

....

DAY

THE HOLY SPIRIT PREPARES PEOPLE TO RECEIVE THE GOSPEL

BY JOSIAH BANCROFT

Josiah Bancroft and his wife Barbara served with Serge in the Republic of Ireland planting churches for eight years and then as senior leaders in the organization for fifteen. Josiah is the author of *Philippians: Finding Joy When Life Is Hard*.

Date: ....

Location: ....

How I'll Be Serving Today: ....

....

....

BIG IDEA

The Spirit leads us to those who are already wanting to hear the gospel.

MEETING WITH GOD *(15 Minutes)*

PHILIP AND THE ETHIOPIAN (ACTS 8:26-40)

²⁶ Now an angel of the Lord said to Philip, "Go south to the road—the desert road—that goes down from Jerusalem to Gaza." ²⁷ So he started out, and on his way he met an Ethiopian eunuch, an important official in charge of all the treasury of the Kandake (which means "queen of the Ethiopians"). This man had gone to Jerusalem to worship, ²⁸ and on his way home was sitting in his chariot reading the Book of Isaiah the prophet. ²⁹ The Spirit told Philip, "Go to that chariot and stay near it."

³⁰ Then Philip ran up to the chariot and heard the man reading Isaiah the prophet. "Do you understand what you are reading?" Philip asked.

³¹ "How can I," he said, "unless someone explains it to me?" So he invited Philip to come up and sit with him.

³² This is the passage of Scripture the eunuch was reading:

"He was led like a sheep to the slaughter,
and as a lamb before its shearer is silent,
so he did not open his mouth.
³³ In his humiliation he was deprived of justice.
Who can speak of his descendants?
For his life was taken from the earth."

³⁴ The eunuch asked Philip, "Tell me, please, who is the prophet talking about, himself or someone else?" ³⁵ Then Philip began with that very passage of Scripture and told him the good news about Jesus.

³⁶ As they traveled along the road, they came to some water and the eunuch said, "Look, here is water. What can stand in the way of my being baptized?" [37] 1 ³⁸ And he gave orders to stop the chariot. Then both Philip and the eunuch went down into the water and Philip baptized him. ³⁹ When they came up out of the water, the Spirit of the Lord suddenly took Philip away, and the eunuch did not see him again, but went on his way rejoicing. ⁴⁰ Philip, however, appeared at Azotus and traveled about, preaching the gospel in all the towns until he reached Caesarea.

---

1. Some manuscripts include here: Philip said, "If you believe with all your heart, you may." The eunuch answered, "I believe that Jesus Christ is the Son of God."

STEP INTO THE FLOW

Think for a second about all the things you did to get ready for your mission trip. You probably had to raise money and recruit a prayer team. You likely had to do some training and learning about the country you were going to, the people you'd be serving, and the work you'd be doing. You may have needed to get a passport, secure visas, and make sure your immunizations were up-to-date. But regardless of what you did, God was also preparing for your trip!

Joining mission work puts you in touch with what the Spirit of God is doing around the world. He is working around the world, drawing people from every tongue and nation to Jesus Christ, and has chosen you to have a part in his mission. To reach the world he will lead you and will speak to hearts through you. Even struggling to enter a new place, learning different ways of speaking, and taking in the culture as an outsider are all things that God uses to spread the gospel. That's remarkable!

But perhaps even more remarkable is the work that his Spirit is doing to prepare people to receive his gospel. He is working in their hearts and their circumstances long before you arrive to open them to his grace. You can expect that he has prepared hearts to respond to the love of Christ as you show them in your example, service, and honest words. Your view of mission will change as you believe that God is preparing those you will meet. Mission becomes anticipation. You're excited to explore where God is at work and how you can join in. Where is God at work? How do I join in?

The Ethiopian eunuch in our passage is a great example of how God prepares people. As a man of position and wealth, he stood out even among the foreigners worshiping in Jerusalem. It is evident that he was trusted with a crucial position in his own country (v. 27). He had a chariot and the available time for travel, which likely further attracted others' attention and curiosity. He received no material benefit from worshipping the God of Israel, so it must have been the work of God's Spirit in his heart that had drawn him to Jerusalem.

The Ethiopian traveled to Jerusalem because it was the one place where God had established his temple and the altar of sacrifice. However, there were hindrances to his pursuit of God. The Jewish worshippers all shared a language, a culture, a heritage, and a way of worship dating back many centuries. The temple even had a physical barrier he could not pass. Jewish temple worshippers moved toward the altar while he could only watch. But God was also making sweeping changes to how his people worshipped after the death and resurrection of Jesus and through the coming of the Spirit at Pentecost.

The Ethiopian left Jerusalem reading a scroll of Isaiah as he continued to feel the urging of God's Spirit. His desire to know more of God left him still seeking. How delighted he must have been that the Spirit sent Philip to him in the desert on his way home to explain the gospel through his reading of Isaiah!

There are many differences between the time of these events and our lives. Yet God still works in the same way. The Spirit prepares hearts, even in the most unlikely of people. Before they understand it, God creates in them a hunger to know him and his love. So whether God sends an angel or uses your faith and circumstances, you can trust that he's working to prepare hearts to hear the good news. You may not see it, but you can believe it, because God has already worked in your own life this way.

When I came to faith, God was at work in my life long before I understood what the Spirit was doing. I had grown up in a respectable, religious family. Yet I had often rebelled against my upbringing. In fact, I was known to give away drugs as a way of gaining friends. But because God loved me, he used my searching and rebellion to help me see my heart's true desires. He brought followers of Christ into my life who helped me see that I wanted what they had: peace, joy, and freedom from guilt.

This is how God works. He orchestrates circumstances and relationships to create something new in us. You can expect that God is already doing that in the people you encounter on your trip. You can take up your part, confidently knowing that God has gone ahead of you.

So what is your part? Letting God speak through you even if you are not the best trained evangelist or most polished speaker. After I came to Christ, when I wanted to share with others, I would take them to my pastor so he could explain the gospel to them. I knew he would help them like he did me. Then one day my pastor said, "Josiah, you don't need to keep bringing people to me. You have the gospel. You have the Spirit. You tell them about Jesus." My pastor was right!

As you join others on mission, you are stepping into the Spirit's flow of taking the gospel to the world. You have good news to share as you partner with a team of long-term missionaries and local believers who are reaching into their community. They have built relationships and have experience you will benefit from during your trip. Their vision and insights will guide your prayers and give you opportunities that will fit your abilities and your time with them. And God will use you uniquely, just as he used Philip to reach the Ethiopian.

As you serve today, you can depend on the Spirit. He will be at work in all kinds of ways. He will use your example, your service, and your sharing to draw people in. They may find new life, or take one step closer to Christ, but regardless of the results you see, God is spreading his good news.

RESPONDING TO GOD *(15 Minutes)*

Philip's interaction with the Ethiopian in today's passage gives us a good model for how to partner with God when we encounter those who don't yet know Jesus.

1. ***First, we can step into any situation expecting God to work.*** Philip is prompted twice by God (vv. 26, 29) in ways that lead him to the Ethiopian. God was already at work in the lives of both Philip and the Ethiopian long before the events of Acts 8.

    - As you think about your trip so far, have you been expecting God to work or struggling to believe that he will? How is this response similar to or different from the way you typically encounter God back home?

- List three places where you have seen clear evidence of God at work on your trip so far.

....

....

....

....

....

....

2. ***Second, we can train our hearts to depend on the Spirit's leading.*** The Holy Spirit wants to guide and prompt you just like he did Philip. Get in the habit of asking, by yourself and with your team, "Spirit, what do you want us to do here?"

- Where have you experienced the Spirit's leading so far on your trip?
- What was your response when you sensed his leading?

....

....

....

....

....

....

3. ***Finally, by asking questions and carefully listening, we can enter their world with curiosity.*** Notice that Philip starts by asking the Ethiopian if he understands the passage from Isaiah. He doesn't

assume that the Ethiopian, who was clearly not Jewish, was stuck and just waiting for Philip to come to the rescue.

- Think of an example from your trip where you made an assumption that ended up being incorrect about people you've come to serve. What happened as a result?
- How could you have entered into that same situation with curiosity instead? What difference do you think that would have made?
- Curiosity and asking questions is a great way to engage with nationals. Not everyone will want to talk with you. But demonstrating that you are there to learn and not "fix" them goes a long way. What can you do to remind yourself of this on the remainder of the trip?

....

....

....

....

....

....

WHAT I SAW GOD DO TODAY

This evening (or tomorrow morning), take a few minutes to record unique ways that you saw God at work. Our sin-hardened hearts easily forget, so writing down a few of the things you've seen God do is a great way to offer thanks and praise to him.

Today I saw God . . .

....

....

....

....

....

....

THE HOLY SPIRIT TRANSFORMS US

BY RACHEL MCLAUGHLIN

Rachel McLaughlin has served with Serge in Kibuye, Burundi, since 2013 as an OB-GYN physician and medical school professor.

Date: ....

Location: ....

How I'll Be Serving Today:..

....

....

BIG IDEA

God can change anyone, no matter what their history or current lifestyle.

MEETING WITH GOD *(15 Minutes)*
SAUL'S CONVERSION (ACTS 9:1–22)

¹Meanwhile, Saul was still breathing out murderous threats against the Lord's disciples. He went to the high priest ²and asked him for letters to the synagogues in Damascus, so that if he found any there who belonged to the Way, whether men or women, he might take them as prisoners to Jerusalem. ³As he neared Damascus on his journey, suddenly a light from heaven flashed around him. ⁴He fell to the ground and heard a voice say to him, "Saul, Saul, why do you persecute me?"

⁵"Who are you, Lord?" Saul asked.

"I am Jesus, whom you are persecuting," he replied. ⁶"Now get up and go into the city, and you will be told what you must do."

⁷The men traveling with Saul stood there speechless; they heard the sound but did not see anyone. ⁸Saul got up from the ground, but when he opened his eyes he could see nothing. So they led him by the hand into Damascus. ⁹For three days he was blind, and did not eat or drink anything.

¹⁰In Damascus there was a disciple named Ananias. The Lord called to him in a vision, "Ananias!"

"Yes, Lord," he answered.

¹¹The Lord told him, "Go to the house of Judas on Straight Street and ask for a man from Tarsus named Saul, for he is praying. ¹²In a vision he has seen a man named Ananias come and place his hands on him to restore his sight."

¹³"Lord," Ananias answered, "I have heard many reports about this man and all the harm he has done to your holy people in Jerusalem. ¹⁴And he has come here with authority from the chief priests to arrest all who call on your name."

¹⁵But the Lord said to Ananias, "Go! This man is my chosen instrument to proclaim my name to the Gentiles and their kings and to the people of Israel. ¹⁶I will show him how much he must suffer for my name."

¹⁷Then Ananias went to the house and entered it. Placing his hands on Saul, he said, "Brother Saul, the Lord—Jesus, who appeared to you on the road as you were coming here—has sent me so that you may see

again and be filled with the Holy Spirit." [18] Immediately, something like scales fell from Saul's eyes, and he could see again. He got up and was baptized, [19] and after taking some food, he regained his strength.

Saul spent several days with the disciples in Damascus. [20] At once he began to preach in the synagogues that Jesus is the Son of God. [21] All those who heard him were astonished and asked, "Isn't he the man who raised havoc in Jerusalem among those who call on this name? And hasn't he come here to take them as prisoners to the chief priests?" [22] Yet Saul grew more and more powerful and baffled the Jews living in Damascus by proving that Jesus is the Messiah.

HOW UNMET EXPECTATIONS CHANGED MY HEART

I had just completed my first year of medical school and was on my way to spend the summer working with a group of Cambodian doctors and nurses on a traveling clinic project. Every Monday morning we would set sail down the Mekong River on a boat and set up clinics twice a day in different villages at the edge of the river. I had very few actual medical skills at that point in my life, but I was dreaming of opportunities to perform life-changing surgery, diagnose incredible diseases, and increase my medical knowledge dramatically.

By the end of day one, I could see that my dreams were not going to come to fruition. I had a difficult time communicating with both staff and patients, who spoke a different language than me. There was no surgery happening in small clinics by the river's edge. I honestly didn't know enough to be of medical assistance, so I ended up playing with local children and counting out pills for the pharmacy to dispense.

That first Friday, when the boat pulled back into the capital city, I returned to the guesthouse and flung myself down on the bed, utterly discouraged. I was frustrated and disappointed with my experience so far, but I still felt compelled to compose a very positive email to my friends and family featuring anecdotes about frogs in the shower buckets and the delicious food I was eating. I felt like if I was honest about not liking everything about my trip, maybe it meant that I wasn't really called to mission work. And that felt unacceptable to me.

Looking back on that summer, now twenty years ago, I can see many ways in which that trip was everything I needed and nothing that I wanted. I wanted my mission career to begin with a bang, to be full of stories and encounters that were all about me and my abilities. What I needed was an experience that would strip away my pride, my self-sufficiency, and my fears about being truly honest. What I needed was more dependence on God—and that's what I ultimately received.

In our reading for today, we see one of the most dramatic conversion experiences ever recorded in the Bible, maybe even of all time. Saul starts out as one of the proverbial bad guys of the New Testament, but with a little delving into his history we see someone who isn't exactly a typical bad guy. Saul is a revered member of the religious community, well trained, well bred, and extremely zealous—just zealous for the wrong thing (Philippians 3:5–6). Saul is so zealous against Christianity that he makes it his life's work to seek out and destroy the Christian church by persecution and murder (Acts 8:3, 9:1–2). God has big plans for this man who would be his chosen vessel to carry the gospel to the entire Gentile world (v. 14). But first, Saul needs some major life transformation. In a flash of light and a thunderous voice, Saul's life is completely changed (vv. 3–4). Everything he holds dear is put into question or taken away from him, even his sight (v. 8). He meets Jesus. He goes from being powerful, celebrated, revered, and honored to being rejected, humiliated, persecuted, and weak. And it is then, and only then, that God can begin to use him.

Many of us don't have a conversion story like Saul. In fact, when it comes time to share personal testimonies, we might shy away from sharing, feeling like however God met us was not "dramatic" enough to be encouraging to anyone. After all, most of us don't need to repent of murdering innocent people. But whether we have been Christians for years or a short amount of time or haven't yet made that commitment in our lives, God still wants to work in us and through us. However, every single one of us has a heart that needs to change first. As I learned in Cambodia and continue to learn every day that I spend overseas, my heart is full of pride, self-centeredness, and contempt for those around me. It has taken me years to realize the truth of Dallas Willard's words: "What God gets out of our lives—and, indeed, what we get out of our lives—is simply the person we become."[2] Yes, God is pleased with our work and our service for him. He delights in working out his purposes for the world through us, broken and sinful vessels. But more than that, he wants our hearts. The Holy Spirit is working in us to make us into the people God intended us to be.

Finally, let's look also to the second person that we are introduced to in Acts 9, Ananias. It's interesting that God chooses this other person to play a key role in Saul's conversion. The only thing Ananias knows about Saul is his terrible reputation (vv. 13–14), but God speaks to Ananias in a vision, inviting him into the story of how God is redeeming his "chosen instrument" (v. 15). Ananias knows of Saul as a powerful, harmful opposer, but his own encounter with Saul is with a broken, blinded man who needs the grace of God. It is Ananias's prayers that healed Saul's blindness and immediately proceeded Saul's baptism (vv. 17–19). Following Jesus's example, Ananias sees not just who Saul had been but who he could become and sacrificially serves him out of love for God.

If we truly believe that God is going to change our hearts as he changed Saul's, we also need to be open to the idea that there will be an Ananias in our own lives. Perhaps God will use a teammate, a supporter or friend back home, or a national partner in your ministry to speak to you. I was resistant to show my weakness in emails to family back home when I served in Cambodia, fearing that my weakness or discouragement would cause others to be disappointed in me. What would it look like for you to be honest not only with yourself, but also with friends and supporters about how your experience is really, truly going? How do you think God could change your heart through the work of his people?

God changed Saul into one of the greatest missionaries the world has ever seen. And he can change each one of us too. I pray that on this trip, the Holy Spirit would continue to show you areas of your heart that need to be revealed and brought into the light and changed. No matter what

---

2. Dallas Willard, *The Divine Conspiracy: Rediscovering Our Hidden Life in God* (New York: HarperCollins, 1998), 275.

those areas are, he has the power to forgive you and to transform you to be more like Jesus.

RESPONDING TO GOD *(15 Minutes)*

Sometimes we think that going on a mission trip will turn us into a "super-Christian." But often it's just the opposite! A Serge missionary once quipped, "Going into missions is like pouring Miracle-Gro® on all your sins."

1. Where has the Holy Spirit been using your trip to show you places in your heart that need to be changed? Pay particular attention to your thoughts, motives, and desires.

....

....

....

....

....

....

2. Most of us assume that as we grow spiritually we will get better and better. It is very disturbing when we begin to see that our sin isn't just limited to our outward actions. It also includes our thoughts, motives, and desires. As we start to see the sinful motives underneath our sinful actions, we often pretend that we are better or holier than we are or perform by trying even harder to be good, at least on the outside. The following chart shows how this stunts our dependence on Christ and his work.

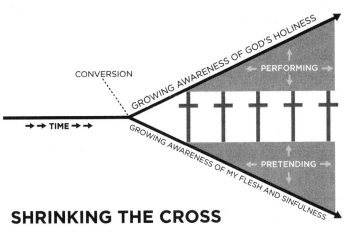

SHRINKING THE CROSS

© 2009 Serge

- Where have you seen yourself pretending on the trip? If you are not sure, ask the Holy Spirit to reveal places where this is happening.
- Where have you seen yourself performing on the trip? If you are not sure, ask the Holy Spirit to reveal places where this is happening.

....

....

....

....

....

....

3. True spiritual growth involves asking God to keep showing us more and more of our sin, so that we can continually develop a deeper appreciation of and reliance on Christ. As this happens, we can be honest about failings instead of trying to cover them by pretending or make up for them by performing. Believing the gospel daily looks

like seeing our sin—internally and externally—more readily, so that we can turn from it more quickly and rely on Jesus more deeply. The following chart shows what it looks like to increasingly rely on Christ and what he accomplished for us on the cross.

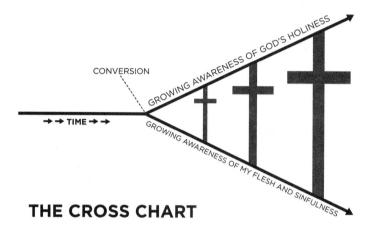

THE CROSS CHART

- As you think about places where you have been pretending or performing, what would it look like to turn from these things?
- What would it look like to rely on Jesus more deeply in these areas? What promises of the gospel would you need to believe more deeply?
- How do you think this should change the way you relate to your team or your national partners?

....

....

....

....

....

....

WHAT I SAW GOD DO TODAY

This evening (or tomorrow morning), take a few minutes to record unique ways that you saw God at work. Our sin-hardened hearts easily forget, so writing down a few of the things you've seen God do is a great way to offer thanks and praise to him.

Today I saw God . . .

THE HOLY SPIRIT BREAKS DOWN DIVISIONS

BY LINDSAY[3]

Lindsay has served in Europe with Serge since 2012. She is passionate about evangelism and enjoys participating in church-planting work among the least-reached peoples of the world.

Date: ....

Location: ....

How I'll Be Serving Today: ....

....

....

BIG IDEA

The good news is for everyone because in God's kingdom there are no insiders or outsiders. Everyone is included.

---

3. Name and details withheld by the author's request due to the sensitive nature of her work.

MEETING WITH GOD *(15 Minutes)*

PETER'S VISION AND VISIT TO CORNELIUS'S HOUSE (ACTS 10:1–43)

¹ At Caesarea there was a man named Cornelius, a centurion in what was known as the Italian Regiment. ² He and all his family were devout and God-fearing; he gave generously to those in need and prayed to God regularly. ³ One day at about three in the afternoon he had a vision. He distinctly saw an angel of God, who came to him and said, "Cornelius!"

⁴ Cornelius stared at him in fear. "What is it, Lord?" he asked.

The angel answered, "Your prayers and gifts to the poor have come up as a memorial offering before God. ⁵ Now send men to Joppa to bring back a man named Simon who is called Peter. ⁶ He is staying with Simon the tanner, whose house is by the sea."

⁷ When the angel who spoke to him had gone, Cornelius called two of his servants and a devout soldier who was one of his attendants. ⁸ He told them everything that had happened and sent them to Joppa.

⁹ About noon the following day as they were on their journey and approaching the city, Peter went up on the roof to pray. ¹⁰ He became hungry and wanted something to eat, and while the meal was being prepared, he fell into a trance. ¹¹ He saw heaven opened and something like a large sheet being let down to earth by its four corners. ¹² It contained all kinds of four-footed animals, as well as reptiles and birds. ¹³ Then a voice told him, "Get up, Peter. Kill and eat."

¹⁴ "Surely not, Lord!" Peter replied. "I have never eaten anything impure or unclean."

¹⁵ The voice spoke to him a second time, "Do not call anything impure that God has made clean."

¹⁶ This happened three times, and immediately the sheet was taken back to heaven.

¹⁷ While Peter was wondering about the meaning of the vision, the men sent by Cornelius found out where Simon's house was and stopped at the gate. ¹⁸ They called out, asking if Simon who was known as Peter was staying there.

[19] While Peter was still thinking about the vision, the Spirit said to him, "Simon, three men are looking for you. [20] So get up and go downstairs. Do not hesitate to go with them, for I have sent them."

[21] Peter went down and said to the men, "I'm the one you're looking for. Why have you come?"

[22] The men replied, "We have come from Cornelius the centurion. He is a righteous and God-fearing man, who is respected by all the Jewish people. A holy angel told him to ask you to come to his house so that he could hear what you have to say." [23] Then Peter invited the men into the house to be his guests.

The next day Peter started out with them, and some of the believers from Joppa went along. [24] The following day he arrived in Caesarea. Cornelius was expecting them and had called together his relatives and close friends. [25] As Peter entered the house, Cornelius met him and fell at his feet in reverence. [26] But Peter made him get up. "Stand up," he said, "I am only a man myself."

[27] While talking with him, Peter went inside and found a large gathering of people. [28] He said to them: "You are well aware that it is against our law for a Jew to associate with or visit a Gentile. But God has shown me that I should not call anyone impure or unclean. [29] So when I was sent for, I came without raising any objection. May I ask why you sent for me?"

[30] Cornelius answered: "Three days ago I was in my house praying at this hour, at three in the afternoon. Suddenly a man in shining clothes stood before me [31] and said, 'Cornelius, God has heard your prayer and remembered your gifts to the poor. [32] Send to Joppa for Simon who is called Peter. He is a guest in the home of Simon the tanner, who lives by the sea.' [33] So I sent for you immediately, and it was good of you to come. Now we are all here in the presence of God to listen to everything the Lord has commanded you to tell us."

[34] Then Peter began to speak: "I now realize how true it is that God does not show favoritism [35] but accepts from every nation the one who fears him and does what is right. [36] You know the message God sent to the people of Israel, announcing the good news of peace through Jesus Christ, who is Lord of all. [37] You know what has happened throughout the province of Judea, beginning in Galilee after the baptism that John preached— [38] how God anointed Jesus of Nazareth with the Holy Spirit

and power, and how he went around doing good and healing all who were under the power of the devil, because God was with him.

[39] "We are witnesses of everything he did in the country of the Jews and in Jerusalem. They killed him by hanging him on a cross, [40] but God raised him from the dead on the third day and caused him to be seen. [41] He was not seen by all the people, but by witnesses whom God had already chosen—by us who ate and drank with him after he rose from the dead. [42] He commanded us to preach to the people and to testify that he is the one whom God appointed as judge of the living and the dead. [43] All the prophets testify about him that everyone who believes in him receives forgiveness of sins through his name."

GOOD NEWS FOR ALL PEOPLE—EXCEPT THEM

Have you ever smelled something that brought you immense joy? It could be the smell of your favorite home-cooked meal, the smell of freshly washed clothes—maybe even the smell of the air after a heavy rainfall (personally, I don't get that one). For me, it's the smell of cedarwood and pine that makes my heart swell with gladness because it makes me think of Christmas. There's something about that smell that sends me into nostalgic bliss as it reminds me of my family and home. It's the best.

It's amazing how much a smell can trigger such deep emotions in us. As we've already seen, this phenomenon can be overwhelmingly positive, but it can also work the opposite way, producing disgust. And disgust, as it so often does, can reveal the deep ugliness of our hearts.

When I was in kindergarten, I had a classmate whose clothes strongly smelled of the food that her family cooked at home. Her family was from a different country, and as a very picky eater at the time, I couldn't fathom ever eating food that created such a smell. I did not like being paired with her for activities, I did not want to sit next to her, and I told myself as a child that not only would I never eat the food that created the smell on her clothes, I also would never go to the country that her family was from. Why? Because it probably smelled too. Nobody taught me this mindset; nobody reinforced it—this attitude came from within my sinful little heart all by myself.

Fast forward fifteen years to me as an eager beaver twenty-one-year-old college graduate who was ready to follow Jesus on mission to the ends of the earth and proclaim his gospel to all peoples. I searched high and low for opportunities to go back to Thailand, which I had visited on a short-term trip a few years prior. Thailand had captured my heart, but I couldn't find a way to get there.

I then went back to the drawing board to find a way to work among unreached peoples in a short-term capacity. I stumbled upon the Serge Apprenticeship and got excited: *Come serve for one to two years* (check!) *among hundreds of thousands of unreached peoples* (check!) *while speaking English* (major check!) *working with people from* . . . wait for it—the country I vowed to never visit.

"No." It was all I could say to God until I sat with the idea for a moment. It was almost as if I could feel the Holy Spirit tapping on my shoulder, whispering in my ear: "Every tribe, every tongue, every nation—do you really believe this?"

I knew God was inviting me to lay down my life for a place and a people that I was not naturally drawn to. I knew that he was inviting me to repent of my sins of racism, cultural prejudice, and pride. I knew that he could change and heal me if I let him. But would I let him?

Before you keep reading, spend a minute answering the first question in the "Responding to God" section below, then continue the devotional reading.

Today in our passage of Acts we meet a man named Cornelius. We learn that Cornelius is a centurion (meaning he is *not* Jewish—this is important) who not only fears God but also gives to the poor (vv. 1–2). We read later that he is also greatly respected by the Jewish people (v. 22), which is no small thing! Cornelius has a vision from God in which he's told to find Peter and listen to what he has to say (v. 5, 22). So in obedience, Cornelius sends out some of his men to go find Peter, who just a day later has a vision from God (three times to be exact!) about animals, a sheet, and a call to "kill and eat!" (v. 13).

Without any context, it would be easy to read about Peter's vision and think not much of it. It seems like he has a strange dream about eating animals. Who doesn't have strange dreams? But this isn't a dream and this vision is about so much more than animals—this is a vision which revealed God's heart to include the Gentiles in his salvation plan. Peter's worldview is getting rocked.

Take a moment and reread verse 14. Here is what I observe:

Peter starts, "Surely not!" which reads to me something like, "Seriously, God?"

And he continues, "I have never eaten anything impure or unclean," which reads to me something like, "I keep the rules, and these are not the rules, God!"

Don't you just love Peter? As was his style, he wears his heart on his sleeve and doesn't hold back from telling God what he thinks. He had been eager and often quite impulsive in defending Jesus (chopping off a man's ear in the garden of Gethsemane ring a bell for anyone?), but often he had missed what Jesus was really doing. I can be a lot like Peter. What about you?

With every verse that we read, we get a glimpse into the power of the Holy Spirit to carry out the purposes of God. In verses 34–35, we find Peter in the house of Cornelius (it was a big deal for a Jewish man to be in a Gentile's home!) proclaiming what God had revealed to him: "I now realize how true it is that God does not show favoritism but accepts from every nation the one who fears him and does what is right."

Imagine the joy of Cornelius and the other Gentiles in the room—this *good* news of great joy was for them, too!

Being faced with our own prejudices and favoritism can be incredibly uncomfortable and even embarrassing—especially if you have been following Jesus for a long time. Earlier I shared with you the internal struggle I faced when I was considering an apprenticeship with Serge. Would

I follow the call of God to lay down my life, my pride, and my prejudice to follow him to a place and a people I was afraid of?

By God's amazing grace, I can say that I did. And next to placing my faith in Jesus as a six-year-old, I can say with confidence—still living and serving in the same place over a decade later—that it was the best decision I have ever made. And you want to know something funny? That same smell which used to be so off-putting to me as a child now makes me feel like I'm home. And the food? I could eat it every day and never grow tired of it. I was the one missing out the whole time.

Much like Cornelius, there are still millions of people all around the world awaiting someone to tell them that the saving work of Jesus is for them too. So can I ask you: Are you ready to step out of your comfort zone and share with them?

RESPONDING TO GOD (15 Minutes)

1. We all harbor prejudice. You may struggle with prejudice toward someone from a different cultural background. Or it could be someone on your mission team on the other side of the political spectrum, or who loves the rival of your favorite sports team.

    • Take a minute to reflect on prejudice in your own life. Is there a group of people who are different from you that you struggle to accept, like, appreciate, or get along with?
    • How have you seen this play out on your trip?

2. Whatever the reason for your prejudice, take a moment to confess your sin and your lack of love for this particular group or type of people before God. Remember—he already knows what's going on in your heart and loves you dearly, so you don't need to be afraid.

3. In our passage today, Peter reminds us that God does not show favoritism but accepts everyone who comes to Christ for salvation. When we see our own need for salvation and recognize that God has welcomed us to his family, our perspective begins to change. Think about the people you identified in question 1, then answer these questions:

    - How is my need for Christ the same as the people I struggle to love?
    - How does Christ's death and resurrection meet both my need and their need for salvation?
    - What does the Holy Spirit need to do in my life to help me love others more?

WHAT I SAW GOD DO TODAY

This evening (or tomorrow morning), take a few minutes to record unique ways that you saw God at work. Our sin-hardened hearts easily forget, so writing down a few of the things you've seen God do is a great way to offer thanks and praise to him.

Today I saw God . . .

....

....

....

....

....

....

THE HOLY SPIRIT HELPS US COMMUNICATE THE GOSPEL IN ANY CONTEXT

BY WADE SAVANT

Wade Savant and his wife Aly served with Serge for eight years, first in the Czech Republic and then in Scotland. Previously, they worked together in ministry in Bolivia and the United States.

Date: ....

Location: ....

How I'll Be Serving Today:...

....

....

BIG IDEA

The gospel meets the need of every person and culture who hears it.

MEETING WITH GOD *(15 Minutes)*
PAUL IN ATHENS (ACTS 17:16–34)

[16] While Paul was waiting for them in Athens, he was greatly distressed to see that the city was full of idols. [17] So he reasoned in the synagogue with both Jews and God-fearing Greeks, as well as in the marketplace day by day with those who happened to be there. [18] A group of Epicurean and Stoic philosophers began to debate with him. Some of them asked, "What is this babbler trying to say?" Others remarked, "He seems to be advocating foreign gods." They said this because Paul was preaching the good news about Jesus and the resurrection. [19] Then they took him and brought him to a meeting of the Areopagus, where they said to him, "May we know what this new teaching is that you are presenting? [20] You are bringing some strange ideas to our ears, and we would like to know what they mean." [21] (All the Athenians and the foreigners who lived there spent their time doing nothing but talking about and listening to the latest ideas.)

[22] Paul then stood up in the meeting of the Areopagus and said: "People of Athens! I see that in every way you are very religious. [23] For as I walked around and looked carefully at your objects of worship, I even found an altar with this inscription: to an unknown god. So you are ignorant of the very thing you worship—and this is what I am going to proclaim to you.

[24] "The God who made the world and everything in it is the Lord of heaven and earth and does not live in temples built by human hands. [25] And he is not served by human hands, as if he needed anything. Rather, he himself gives everyone life and breath and everything else. [26] From one man he made all the nations, that they should inhabit the whole earth; and he marked out their appointed times in history and the boundaries of their lands. [27] God did this so that they would seek him and perhaps reach out for him and find him, though he is not far from any one of us. [28] 'For in him we live and move and have our being.' As some of your own poets have said, 'We are his offspring.'

[29] "Therefore since we are God's offspring, we should not think that the divine being is like gold or silver or stone—an image made by human design and skill. [30] In the past God overlooked such ignorance, but now

he commands all people everywhere to repent. [31] For he has set a day when he will judge the world with justice by the man he has appointed. He has given proof of this to everyone by raising him from the dead."

[32] When they heard about the resurrection of the dead, some of them sneered, but others said, "We want to hear you again on this subject." [33] At that, Paul left the Council. [34] Some of the people became followers of Paul and believed. Among them was Dionysius, a member of the Areopagus, also a woman named Damaris, and a number of others.

BECOMING CULTURAL CHAMELEONS

As we sat down to chat with a group of international friends and I began to talk, I could feel my wife's internal eye roll aimed in my direction.

He's doing it again, I could tell she was thinking to herself. And she was right.

My wife and I both grew up in the American South where accents come thick as honey. But something strange has happened to me over the years of our living in various countries and continents. My voice has changed, and as best as I can understand, my accent has become either neutralized or imitative of the person with whom I am speaking. Nowadays, I'm more likely to be mistaken as someone from the British Isles than someone who was born in the low country of South Carolina.

Some of that change was subconscious and subtle, an internal response to years of listening to people whose native language or manner of speaking was different from mine. Some of the change can be attributed to learning the languages spoken in our various countries of residence, which slowed down how I spoke—and even thought—in my native tongue.

But certainly, some of the change in my speech is conscious and intentional. It is born of a realization that if I speak as quickly and colloquially to my Bolivian, Czech, or Scottish friends as I do to my childhood Carolina friends, then I will be unintelligible. The context of where I am or to whom I am speaking directs the phrases I choose and how I say them. I must adapt the method of my speech to be heard well.

In our passage, Paul models something very similar (but much deeper!) as he engages with the Athenian culture and peoples. His *motive* is the same as every place he visited: to see the lost reconciled to God through repentance and faith (v. 30). The core of his *message* is unchanged: the resurrection of Jesus confirms that he is Lord over all (vv. 18, 31). But the *method* of how he reaches the intellectual elite of Athens is adjusted to their context. What Paul sees as he walked around the city, waiting for his friends to join him, informs both where he went and how he spoke.

It's important to understand that this was not a coincidence but rather a pattern that Paul employs throughout his missionary journeys. In Acts 13, while preaching to a group of deeply religious Jews at Pisidian Antioch, Paul shapes the content of his sermon to show that the resurrection of Jesus was the fulfillment of all the longings of Old Testament history and Scripture. So also, when speaking to a group of pagans at Lystra in Acts 14, Paul adapts his message in a way that communicates the truth about God in relatable terms to his listeners.

In other words, we are seeing Paul live out what he wrote in 1 Corinthians 9:19–23:

> Though I am free and belong to no one, I have made myself a slave to everyone, to win as many as possible. To the Jews I became like a Jew, to win the Jews. To those under the law I became like one under the law (though I myself am not under the law), so as to win those under the law. To those not having the law I became like one not having the law (though I am not free from God's law but am under Christ's law), so as to win those not having the law. To the weak I became weak, to win the weak. I have become all things to all people so that by all possible means I might save some. I do all this for the sake of the gospel, that I may share in its blessings.

This is a remarkable passage, made even more remarkable by the fact that we are able to witness Paul doing these very things in Acts. But what enables *us* to become such cultural chameleons as Paul, humbly listening, learning, and adapting to others? It is only as we are molded by the gospel that we will be able to set aside our preconceived notions of what our ministry should look like and instead be willing to "become all things for all people" (1 Corinthians 9:22).

God owes us nothing. His holiness means he is free and belongs to no one. And yet, he has lavished his love upon us. In Christ, *he* became like *us*, taking on flesh and bone, born under the law, even becoming sin, so that his people would be set free. He did all of this to be with you, because although he owes you nothing, he loves you and longs to be with you!

In the same way, the freedom Paul has in the gospel does not lead to disinterest in the spiritually dead people of Athens or their culture. Rather than being put off by their rampant idolatry, he sees their deep need and moves in, even as his spirit is distressed (v. 16). He is willing to go beyond his regular practice of preaching in the synagogues to meet the people where they are, mixing and talking in the cultural milieu of the marketplace (v. 17). Once invited to speak at the Areopagus, he uses the Athenians' own words, literature, and instinctive longings for God in his gospel message (vv. 21–22). He listens to learn how best to speak. He is sensitive to their values yet challenges their unbelief and the places where sin has twisted their ability to see clearly. In short, he is a man whose conviction is that the gospel of Jesus Christ fulfills the ultimate longings of every person and culture.

Would Paul's message to the religious Jews in Acts 13 have worked as well if he preached it in Athens? We can't be sure, but I suspect it would not have had the same effect. And simply adapting well to the context will not ensure revival or a smashing success—we see some Athenians still publicly mock Paul (v. 32). But, wonderfully, others are drawn to the gospel and come to faith.

The truth is that we're all products of certain cultures (family, race, nationality, etc.), and we carry those aspects of ourselves wherever we go. But the beauty of God's diverse creativity in that respect becomes endangered when we believe that our perspectives or practices are the only right way to view the world. Becoming a cultural chameleon does not mean compromising the truth of the gospel, but being humble enough to be a servant to all, to learn how best to communicate God's love to others, to win as many as possible.

Because after all, this is what Jesus has done for you.

RESPONDING TO GOD *(15 Minutes)*

1. What have been the biggest cultural differences between your home culture and the host culture where you are ministering?

    - Which of these differences have been refreshing and enjoyable?
    - Which of them have been difficult or unpleasant?

    ....

    ....

    ....

    ....

    ....

    ....

2. Where have you had to make changes to the way you normally operate in order to better love the people you have come to serve?

    - Where have you struggled to do this (even if no one else can tell)?
    - What have you learned by having to change your mindset or actions?

    ....

    ....

    ....

....

....

....

3. Loving people who don't look like us, act like us, or think like us is
    one of the most difficult things we can do. Yet like Paul we are called
    to "become all things for all people" for the sake of the gospel. In
    the Responding to God section of Day 2, you were introduced to the
    five-minute drill on page 31.

    - Have you been using the drill? If so, what have you been learn-
      ing? If not, where could you use it in the next few days?
    - Think of a person you have been struggling to love or an aspect
      of your ministry during your trip where you have been moti-
      vated by duty or guilt instead of love for Jesus. What would it
      look like to use the five-minute drill the next time you are in this
      situation?

....

....

....

....

....

....

WHAT I SAW GOD DO TODAY

This evening (or tomorrow morning), take a few minutes to record
unique ways that you saw God at work. Our sin-hardened hearts easily
forget, so writing down a few of the things you've seen God do is a great
way to offer thanks and praise to him.

Today I saw God . . .

....

....

....

....

....

....

THE HOLY SPIRIT CONTINUES TO WORK TODAY

BY ERIC MCLAUGHLIN

Eric McLaughlin has served with Serge in Burundi since 2013 as a missionary physician and medical school professor. Eric is a Zenger Prize winner for one of his contributions to *Christianity Today* and the author of *Promises in the Dark: Walking with Those in Need Without Losing Heart*.

Date: ....

Location: ....

How I'll Be Serving Today: ....

....

....

BIG IDEA

Many times on mission, things don't go as planned, but the gospel always moves forward.

MEETING WITH GOD *(15 Minutes)*
PAUL PREACHES AT ROME UNDER GUARD
(ACTS 28:23–31)

²³ They arranged to meet Paul on a certain day, and came in even larger numbers to the place where he was staying. He witnessed to them from morning till evening, explaining about the kingdom of God, and from the Law of Moses and from the Prophets he tried to persuade them about Jesus. ²⁴ Some were convinced by what he said, but others would not believe. ²⁵ They disagreed among themselves and began to leave after Paul had made this final statement: "The Holy Spirit spoke the truth to your ancestors when he said through Isaiah the prophet:

> ²⁶ "'Go to this people and say,
> "You will be ever hearing but never understanding;
>   you will be ever seeing but never perceiving."
> ²⁷ For this people's heart has become calloused;
>   they hardly hear with their ears,
>   and they have closed their eyes.
> Otherwise they might see with their eyes,
>   hear with their ears,
>   understand with their hearts
>   and turn, and I would heal them.'

²⁸ "Therefore I want you to know that God's salvation has been sent to the Gentiles, and they will listen!" [29]⁴

³⁰ For two whole years Paul stayed there in his own rented house and welcomed all who came to see him. ³¹ He proclaimed the kingdom of God and taught about the Lord Jesus Christ—with all boldness and without hindrance!

---

4. Some manuscripts include here "After he said this, the Jews left, arguing vigorously among themselves."

LOOKING BACK AND WONDERING WHAT JUST HAPPENED

Think about the hopes that you brought into this journey. What did you hope would happen during this time? What possible outcomes made this trip worth undertaking?

As you now near the end of this trip, what has come of those hopes? Have your expectations been realized? Maybe they haven't. For any number of reasons, perhaps you are quite disappointed. Maybe your own short-comings have even come into the mix. Maybe you are asking yourself if going on this trip was a mistake.

On the other hand, maybe your time of service has been great, even exceeding your expectations, and you are filled with joy.

Whether you are feeling your hopes gratified or dashed, let me remind you that you do not know the whole story. Truly, you can't. All that seems accomplished could fall apart in the months (if not weeks) after your departure. Maybe the project you think you finished comes undone a few days after you leave. On the other hand, what you see as a disappointment may indeed be a seed planted in someone—perhaps someone who wasn't even the focus of your ministry efforts. Unbeknownst to you, this seed could bear great fruit in decades to come. We simply don't know.

We go out to serve and to, in some small way, advance the kingdom of our Lord. How do we face the uncertainty of what's next, when our part of the work is done?

There is a beautifully prosaic ambiguity to these final verses of the book of Acts. After miracles, shipwrecks, high discourse before eminent per-sonalities, and a rapidly growing group of people putting their faith in Jesus the Messiah, Luke gives us an incredibly ordinary finale. Paul finally gets to Rome, where he remains under arrest (vv. 11–16), and he does what he had always done. He reaches out to Jews and then Gentiles, telling his story and seeking to convince them that Jesus is their only hope (vv. 17–22).

And what is the visible result? Well, not much. People come to visit him. Some are convinced; some are not (v. 24). There are mini victories and mini setbacks, but there is no storytelling like in the previous chapters, because there really isn't much of a story to tell. Note that this segment is describing "two whole years" (v. 30). We are left with the impression that this part is included because it brings us up to the time of Luke's writing; otherwise, it might have been skipped or perhaps summed up simply as "Paul spent two years there."

Imagine that we had the chance to ask Paul the same question that I opened with. "Paul, how do you feel about these last two years compared to what you hoped would happen?" What would he say?

In my mind, he pauses to think, and then starts running his mental list: "Well, there have been some good things. But there have been some really hard hearts where not much seems to have happened. And I'm still in these chains, and I'm not really sure what all this waiting is for."

But based on Paul's overall character, I think he would finally come around to something like: "Who knows? God knows. He is the Lord and his kingdom goes forward. Am I planting or watering? I am not always sure, but that doesn't really matter, because God is the one who gives the increase (1 Corinthians 3:6). Jesus told us that his kingdom is like a seed in the ground, growing whether we work or sleep, in a way that we can't even comprehend (Mark 4:26–29). We try and figure these things out, but we can't. God's kingdom is God's kingdom, not ours. It's too big for us to manage or even evaluate properly. I can't even judge myself (1 Corinthians 4:3). I am called simply to be faithful to my Savior and trust in his bigger and better hands."

How do you really quantify the sum total of your trip? Based on what you observe, should you be grateful for what you experienced, or should you be disappointed that it wasn't something more? In the end, because every ministry experience is always a mix of the good and the bad, you could lean either way. In most cases, your response—either gratitude or complaint—is not purely dictated by your circumstances. In one way or another, you get to choose how you respond.

Luke models this choice by ending an arguably underwhelming passage with a surprise exclamation point: "He proclaimed the kingdom of God and taught about the Lord Jesus Christ—with all boldness and without hindrance!" (v. 31). Paul's time in Rome was a mixed bag, like life always is. But thank God that Paul had truth in his words, boldness in his heart, and no hindrance in his preaching (despite all the other hindrances in his circumstances). Thank God that Paul was faithful to his Savior, regardless of the visible fruit.

No matter what happened on this trip, you can rejoice that God loves those you have come to serve more than you ever could. Thank God that his seeds in your own heart are growing—in ways you can't even imagine. And you can trust that he will grow the seeds of the gospel in others' hearts for his glory, even if you never know the whole story.

Here at the end of this journey, you can wonder what really took place. It's hard to know, but you *can* know that there are good reasons for gratitude.

It is natural to gauge our sense of failure or success by how closely the outcome meets our expectations. Russell Moore, writing of the early years of his marriage, offers a helpful parallel, confessing, "what it meant for [something] to be 'good' . . . would be for it to go according to my own plan. I was deeply and profoundly stupid."[5] In missions, what seems good and right to us may not come about, but that may be the best possible outcome. There is a freedom in relinquishing these expectations—this leads us to rest in his peace. Because our Father is always at work, letting go of our preconceived expectations leads us to hope in something better than what we had imagined.

We are called to serve and sacrifice and to do so well, wisely, and winsomely. By grace, we are brought into the work of building God's kingdom. But we are children, and this work thankfully rests on our Father, not on us. We have but one task, which is to awake each day and be faithful to our Savior.

---

5. Russell Moore, *The Storm-Tossed Family: How the Cross Reshapes the Home* (Nashville: B&H Publishing Group, 2018), 133.

RESPONDING TO GOD *(15 Minutes)*

1. There are several questions at the start of this book. Spend a few minutes answering them now:

    - What did you hope would happen during this time?
    - What possible outcomes made this trip worth undertaking?
    - As you now near the end, what has come about?
    - Have your expectations been realized?

    ....

    ....

    ....

    ....

    ....

    ....

2. The Holy Spirit was at work in your life, and the lives of those you ministered to, long before your trip and will remain at work long after the trip as well.

    - How do you want him to continue to work in your life when you get home?
    - How do you want him to continue to work in the lives of those you've met on your trip?

    ....

    ....

    ....

    ....

    ....

3. God's kingdom is too big and wide and deep for any of us to really get our minds around. On this side of heaven, we will only ever experience a few pieces of it at a time. But the parts that we see and experience are real—perhaps the most real thing most of us will ever encounter in this life because they will continue to grow and last into eternity.

    - As you finish up your trip, where have you caught a glimpse of God making all things new?
    - How have these experiences changed the way you see God?
    - How have they changed the way you see yourself?

    ....

    ....

    ....

    ....

    ....

    ....

Note: You'll have a chance to think through these types of questions more deeply in Debrief One: Making Sense of What You've Seen (page 121) after your trip.

WHAT I SAW GOD DO TODAY

This evening (or tomorrow morning), take a few minutes to record unique ways that you saw God at work. Our sin-hardened hearts easily forget, so writing down a few of the things you've seen God do is a great way to offer thanks and praise to him.

Today I saw God . . .

....

....

....

....

....

....

ADDITIONAL DEVOTIONAL RESOURCE
Introducing *Lectio Divina*[6]

Not every mission trip fits neatly into ten days. For those who will be doing a longer trip or simply want a change of pace from the standard devotions, I recommend that you try your hand at something called *lectio divina*.

Lectio divina (literally "divine reading") is a devotional way of reading Scripture that dates back to at least the twelfth century. It *slowly* approaches the biblical text in a way that helps us to really *hear* what it's saying, to *personalize* the text to our unique situations, to respond to God in *prayer*, and to *live* out the text. Many times we read Scripture too fast and superficially; we need to slow down. *Lectio divina* can be compared to enjoying a nourishing three-course meal at your favorite restaurant instead of speeding through a meal from a fast food place.

There are four parts to this method of approaching Scripture.

1. *Lectio:* **The slow reading of the text.** As you approach the Scripture passage, take time to read it aloud (or silently to yourself). Treat the text as a letter directly written to you. Reflect on what you have read; don't rush. Listen to the gentle whisper of God speaking to you (1 Kings 19:12). Read it through two or three times, spending some time in silence between readings. Read until you find a particular word, phrase, or theme that captures your attention. This could be a word of comfort *or* disruption.

---

6. This introduction to *lectio divina* is adapted from *Gospel Growth: Becoming a Faith-Filled Person* by Serge. To order copies of this study or other Serge materials, visit New Growth Press: newgrowthpress.com.

2. *Meditatio:* **Meditating on the text.** Here you focus on the particular words, phrase, or theme that stood out in your reading. This meditating is pondering or ruminating on one particular part of the text. Repeat to yourself the portion of text; perhaps even memorize it. As you meditate on it, how does it speak to you—to your hopes, fears, or desires? What thoughts or memories come to mind? What is God saying to you this moment, on this day? What is God telling you about himself, about yourself, about your situation, or about people you know?

3. *Oratio:* **Praying the text.** The passage now serves as the basis for a conversation with your Father. Talk to him about what's on your heart and what your meditation has brought to your attention. Your prayer is now your response to God, based on what you have read and meditated on. This may include thanks, questions, frustrations, praise, requests, or confession of sin.

4. *Contemplatio:* **Putting the text into practice.** Although this word sounds passive, this step emphasizes putting the text into action. We must now live the passage. This may be described as restful activity! It is living before God and enjoying his presence. Here you take what you have read, meditated on, and prayed, and now go and live it. This is the full reception of the text, the incarnation of the text in your life—living it before God.

USING *LECTIO DIVINA*

To use the *lectio divina* devotional reading process, simply choose a passage of Scripture and work through each of the steps listed above. You don't need to go in order; some days you may spend more time in one or two elements of the process than you do in others.

It helps to choose just a few verses rather than a longer passage, so that you can really sit with each verse. As much as you can, slow down. Rest. Think. Absorb. And talk with God as you do.

LECTIO DIVINA READING ONE

Date: ....

Location: ....

Passage: ....

1. *Lectio:* **Slowly read the text two or three times.**

    What words, phrases, or ideas capture your attention?

    ....

    ....

    ....

    ....

    ....

    ....

2. *Meditatio:* **Meditate on the text.**

    What is God saying to you through these verses? What is he inviting you to? What assurance is he giving you?

    ....

    ....

    ....

    ....

    ....

    ....

3. *Oratio:* **Pray the text.**

   What do you need to say to God in light of what you hear him saying to you in the passage?

   ....

   ....

   ....

   ....

   ....

   ....

4. *Contemplatio:* **Put the text into practice.**

   As you think about your day, what is God calling you to?

   ....

   ....

   ....

   ....

   ....

   ....

LECTIO DIVINA READING TWO

Date: ....

Location: ....

Passage: ....

1. *Lectio:* **Slowly read the text two or three times.**

    What words, phrases, or ideas capture your attention?

    ....

    ....

    ....

    ....

    ....

2. *Meditatio:* **Meditate on the text.**

    What is God saying to you through these verses? What is he inviting you to? What assurance is he giving you?

    ....

    ....

    ....

    ....

    ....

3. *Oratio:* **Pray the text.**

    What do you need to say to God in light of what you hear him saying to you in the passage?

    ....

    ....

    ....

    ....

    ....

4. *Contemplatio:* **Put the text into practice.**

    As you think about your day, what is God calling you to?

    ....

    ....

    ....

    ....

    ....

    ....

LECTIO DIVINA READING THREE

Date: ....

Location: ....

Passage: ....

1. *Lectio:* **Slowly read the text two or three times.**

    What words, phrases, or ideas capture your attention?

    ....

    ....

    ....

    ....

    ....

    ....

2. *Meditatio:* **Meditate on the text.**

What is God saying to you through these verses? What is he inviting you to? What assurance is he giving you?

....

....

....

....

....

3. *Oratio:* **Pray the text.**

What do you need to say to God in light of what you hear him saying to you in the passage?

....

....

....

....

....

4. *Contemplatio:* **Put the text into practice.**

As you think about your day, what is God calling you to?

....

....

....

....

....

LECTIO DIVINA READING FOUR

Date: ....

Location: ....

Passage: ....

1. *Lectio:* **Slowly read the text two or three times.**

   What words, phrases, or ideas capture your attention?

   ....

   ....

   ....

   ....

   ....

   ....

2. *Meditatio:* **Meditate on the text.**

   What is God saying to you through these verses? What is he inviting you to? What assurance is he giving you?

   ....

   ....

   ....

   ....

   ....

   ....

3. *Oratio:* **Pray the text.**

   What do you need to say to God in light of what you hear him saying to you in the passage?

   ....

   ....

   ....

   ....

   ....

   ....

4. *Contemplatio:* **Put the text into practice.**

   As you think about your day, what is God calling you to?

   ....

   ....

   ....

   ....

   ....

   ....

LECTIO DIVINA READING FIVE

Date: ....

Location: ....

Passage: ....

1. *Lectio:* **Slowly read the text two or three times.**

   What words, phrases, or ideas capture your attention?

   ....

   ....

   ....

   ....

   ....

2. *Meditatio:* **Meditate on the text.**

   What is God saying to you through these verses? What is he inviting you to? What assurance is he giving you?

   ....

   ....

   ....

   ....

   ....

3. *Oratio:* **Pray the text.**

   What do you need to say to God in light of what you hear him saying to you in the passage?

   ....

   ....

   ....

   ....

   ....

4. *Contemplatio:* **Put the text into practice.**

As you think about your day, what is God calling you to?

....

....

....

....

....

....

TRAVELOGUE FEATURES

OUR JOURNEY

Whether you go halfway around the world or over to the next state, some of your team's most memorable moments will be made on the way to and from the field. As you travel, take a few minutes to record what happened on each leg of your journey. Be sure to record all of those unique travel memories—rushing to make a connection, juggling immense amounts of luggage and supplies, running into unexpected delays, making a new friend while waiting in line, or trying to sleep in the train station. These are things that seem really crazy in the moment but will become memories that make you laugh when you return.

To the Field		
Leg 1	**Leg 2**	**Leg 3**

Date:

From:

To:

Mode of Travel:

Distance:

To the Field		
Leg 4	**Leg 5**	**Leg 6**
Date:		
From:		
To:		
Mode of Travel:		
Distance:		

From the Field		
Leg 1	**Leg 2**	**Leg 3**
Date:		
From:		
To:		
Mode of Travel:		
Distance:		

From the Field		
Leg 4	Leg 5	Leg 6

Date:

From:

To:

Mode
of Travel:

Distance:

TRAVEL MEMORIES

....

....

....

....

....

....

....

NEW FRIENDS

One of the best parts of any mission trip is the new friends you make. They could be the missionaries you are coming to help, people from other groups and churches who team up to serve with you, national believers you end up working with, or a host family that welcomes you.

Throughout your trip, each time you meet special people you didn't know before, make note of them. Include where or how you met and some contact information if you'd like to be able to connect with them later.

Name	How You Met	Contact Info

Name	How You Met	Contact Info

MISSION MEMORIES

Every trip creates unique memories that you'll want to capture while they are still fresh so that you can share them with others or relive them in future years. Do your best to record things as they happen or grab a few teammates and work through the list toward the end of your time. Don't worry if you don't have an answer for every question. If something particularly memorable happened, be sure to jot that down too.

1. I shared a room with:

....

....

....

2. The funniest thing that happened on the trip:

....

....

....

3. The best food I ate:

....

....

....

4. The worst/scariest thing I ate:

....

....

....

5. Who gets the award for:

    • Heaviest Luggage

    ....

    • Most Unique "Hidden" Skill Set

    ....

    • Most Memorable "I Can't Believe He/She Did That" Moment

    ....

    • Hardest Worker

    ....

    • Best Encourager

    ....

    • Most Adventurous Eater

    ....

6. Which of the people you served really stood out to you? Why?

    ....

    ....

    ....

7. Your most unusual experience:

    ....

    ....

    ....

8. The biggest surprise about the people you came to serve:

    ....

....

....

9. The biggest surprise about your team:

....

....

....

10. If your trip had a theme song, what would it be? Why?

....

....

....

11. What is something that you "had to be there" to truly understand?

....

....

....

12. The "quote of the trip" (what was said and by whom):

....

....

....

13. The biggest challenge you faced:

....

....

....

14. The most unexpected thing that made you grateful (eventually):

....

....

....

BY THE NUMBERS

You'd be surprised at just how many things God brings together to make mission trips possible. Do your best to fill out all of the entries, even if you have to make a few educated guesses. Seeing all of the facts and figures that went into your trip is always enlightening.

1. Number of months spent preparing and planning for the trip:
   ....

2. Amount of support needed for the trip: ....

3. Number of people who gave to you and/or prayed for you: ....

4. Number of people on your team from your church: ....

5. Total number of people on the trip: ....

6. Number of days the trip took: ....

7. Total number of miles traveled: ....

8. Number of people served on the trip: ....

9. Number of hours spent serving others on the trip (i.e., spent in "ministry time"): ....

10. Number of types of transportation you used: ....

11. Number of fast food meals eaten: ....

12. Number of cities/states/countries you traveled over or through:
    ....

13. Number of people you thought would never finish the trip:
    ....

AFTER THE TRIP

THE TRIP IS DONE!

Congratulations! You've survived! You're home—or nearly there!

Over the last several months you've raised support, planned, prepared, and hopefully had a great experience loving and serving others while you were away.

But in many ways, the real work of your mission trip is just now beginning. Finding ways to take what you learned and experienced on the trip and connecting it to your everyday life is crucial for all short-term mission experiences. Unless you are intentional about this, the spiritual lessons and passions awakened by the trip will fade with your memories of your experiences. Despite the time, effort, and expense involved, it's likely that your trip will feel like little more than a week of work unless you set aside time to reflect, process, and talk with God about it.

In light of that, I encourage you to think of the three debrief exercises that follow as *one of the most important parts of your mission experience*. They will help you process what you've experienced and capture the key things God has shown you. They will also invite you to prayerfully consider how Jesus wants to draw you deeper into his mission of redeeming and restoring a lost and broken world. And they will give you suggestions on how to live on mission now that you are back.

Take a few minutes right now to look through your calendar and pencil in dates to complete each debrief. Plan on spending roughly forty-five minutes on each session.

DEBRIEF ONE | MAKING SENSE OF WHAT YOU'VE SEEN

Debrief One focuses on your experiences on the trip and the key things you learned while both are still fresh in your mind.

Debrief One should be completed on your way home or within the first week of your return.

I'll complete Debrief One on: ....

DEBRIEF TWO | THE GOSPEL IN AND THROUGH YOU TO OTHERS

Debrief Two focuses on the lessons you learned, the passions you developed, and how they connect with your everyday life to help you continue living on mission.

Debrief Two should be completed four to six weeks after your return.

I'll complete Debrief Two on: ....

DEBRIEF THREE | THE ONGOING JOURNEY

Debrief Three will help you review your plan and suggest other, long-term ways to keep staying engaged with missions and local outreach.

Debrief Three should be completed six months after you have returned.

I'll complete Debrief Three on: ....

God was at work in your life long before you ever left, and he'll continue to be at work in the days and months ahead, but your mission trip represents a unique opportunity for spiritual growth and engagement. I hope you'll give yourself the gift of spending some time talking with God about what he's done in you and asking him how he'd like to continue to work through you.

DEBRIEF ONE | MAKING SENSE OF WHAT YOU'VE SEEN

Timeframe for Completion: On the way home or during your first week back

INTRODUCTION

Remember the spectrum of emotions you felt as you prepared for your trip a few weeks ago? As you reenter your home culture and the routines of "normal life," you may be experiencing a similar whirlwind of feelings.

Use the following journaling assignment to reflect on your trip and identify the insights you've gained about yourself, about God, and about mission. Taking this intentional time of reflection will be a crucial first step in connecting your short-term trip to your life back home. It will serve you well as you tell others what happened during your week of ministry.

PART 1. EXPECTATIONS AND REALITY

Read your responses from *Part 1: Inventory of Needs and Hopes* (page 6) in the Pre-Trip Assignments, then answer the following questions. Be as specific as you can, citing particular incidents, locations, and people. Use this book's devotional and journaling sections to jog your memory if needed.

1. What were your biggest fears or struggles going into the trip?

....

....

....

....

....

- What actually happened on the trip in these areas?

....

....

....

....

2. What were your biggest hopes or desires for how God would work on the trip?

....

....

....

....

....

....

- What actually happened on the trip in these areas?

....

....

....

....

PART 2. WHAT DID YOU LEARN ABOUT YOURSELF?

As you reflect on what you learned about yourself during the trip, answer the following questions:

1. Where did you feel like you had "poured Miracle-Gro®" on your sin during the trip? (See if you can list a specific incident or sin pattern.) What did this reveal to you about the ongoing level of unbelief that is present in your heart?

....

....

....

....

....

....

2. When was the most significant time you had to step out in faith to
do something on the trip?

....

....

....

....

....

....

- What were you feeling before you did it?

....

....

....

....

- How did God meet you?

....

....

....

....

- What happened as a result?

....

....

....

....

3. Think of a few times when you saw God specifically use you on the trip. It could have been by helping or encouraging a teammate, loving one of the people you came to serve, or giving you the solution to a difficult problem or situation.

- What happened?

....

....

....

....

- What was it like to experience God using you in this way?

....

....

....

....

PART 3. WHAT DID YOU LEARN ABOUT GOD?

Getting to see God work in us and through us in unexpected and exciting ways is one of the great experiences of a mission trip. Take ten or fifteen minutes now to sit and listen to God, considering the following question. Be patient and listen for his voice, recording whatever things the Holy Spirit brings to mind.

God, in light of all that you did and showed me on the trip, what do you want to say to me right now that I should remember as I reengage my normal life?

GETTING READY TO TELL YOUR STORY

In the coming days and weeks, many will want to hear about your mission experience. Different people will want to hear about your trip in varying degrees of depth. Using your reflections above, spend a few minutes writing a one-minute version, a five-minute version, and a twenty-minute version of your experience.

I'd also recommend asking a trusted friend to meet with you for an hour so that you can run through your different summaries and process things out loud. You may find that you've forgotten to include important elements, or that some parts of your experience are best kept private. Having talked through your trip with a close friend can also help if you are nervous about telling others about your trip.

Key details for a twenty-minute story

....

....

....

....

Key details for a five-minute story

....

....

....

....

Key details for a one-minute story

....

....

....

DON'T FORGET to write a note to your support team, thanking them for their generosity and their prayers. Be sure to include a few of the insights that you wrote down in the previous sections.

DEBRIEF TWO | THE GOSPEL IN AND THROUGH YOU TO OTHERS

Timeframe for Completion: Four to six weeks after returning

INTRODUCTION

By now the dust has settled, the suitcases are (hopefully!) unpacked, jet lag is over, and life likely feels "back to normal." As you process the difference between everyday life and "that trip I took a month ago," use the following journaling exercises to consider these questions: Now that I'm home, how do I engage differently with my own heart and my need for the gospel? And with the world's needs?

Note to Leaders: Now would be a great time for a group reunion and debrief. You could incorporate the plans people will be developing in Part 2 (below) into the group conversation, and help those with similar passions to connect with each other.

PART 1. THE GOSPEL IN ME (JOURNALING EXERCISE)

One of the gifts of short-term mission is the opportunity to see our sin and neediness more clearly. Your time in cross-cultural ministry probably revealed some deep heart-level needs that you may have never noticed before—needs that were always there but hard to see in your everyday life.

1. As I consider the spiritual needs I felt during my trip, where do I see similar strands of unbelief now, in my life back home? What new corners of neediness do I see in my heart?

....

....

....

....

....

....

2. How is Jesus meeting me in the midst of these struggles? What specific things can I receive from the gospel as I face unbelief in my life right now?

....

....

....

....

....

....

PART 2. THE GOSPEL THROUGH ME (JOURNALING + PLANNING EXERCISE)

It always seems easier to reach out to those who don't know Jesus when we are on a mission trip. After all, that's why "we" came—to serve "them." But the truth is that when we are following Jesus's lead on how to love people, there is no "us" and "them." There is only "us"—people who desperately need Jesus, every day, to be their Savior, to lead and guide, to heal and empower. Some of us know this, some of us don't. But we are all sinners in need of a Savior. After all, being a Christian doesn't remove your need for Jesus; it simply shows you how amazingly he meets that need.

One lasting impact of every mission trip should be a greater desire and ability to live on mission as part of our everyday lives. Take some time to think through the following questions. As you do, really pray and really listen to what God is saying. It may be helpful to recall a time on your trip when you felt totally helpless but then saw God answer your prayers and meet your needs in clear and overwhelming ways.

1. What needs do I see in the world around me? In my church? In my neighborhood? In my social circles? In my workplace? In the world?

....

....

....

....

....

2. Where might God be calling me into mission back home in deeper ways?

   For each category below, try to list one or two concrete actions that you sense God is calling you to do. Then share your list with a few friends and ask them to pray for you.

   If you need suggestions for what action steps look like in each heading, see the Practical Helps list at the end of Debrief Two.

   God, how are you drawing me to **pray** differently?

....

....

....

God, where are you calling me to **serve** more intentionally?

....

....

....

....

God, where are you encouraging me to **give** more generously?

....

....

....

....

God, where are you asking me to **go** boldly?

....

....

....

....

PART 3. JESUS WITH ME (JOURNALING EXERCISE)

1. What feels challenging and risky about the plan I created? How is this pushing me to be more dependent on Jesus? Just as I got ready for my short-term trip and felt needy, how do I feel needy now, as I get ready to step deeper into mission in my local context?

....

....

....

....

....

2. How does the gospel speak to my specific fears and needs?

Pray for Jesus to meet you here; pray for his partnership as you come alongside him in loving the lost.

....

....

....

....

....

PRACTICAL HELPS

We've brainstormed a starter list of ways you may want to consider praying, serving, giving, and going. Feel free to use this as a jumping-off point as you create your plan in Part 2 above, but don't feel limited to choosing things from the lists. God can use you any way he wants!

Continue Learning

- *Now that you have firsthand knowledge of a new part of the world, keep exploring.* Read a book, watch a movie, or visit a museum that will help you keep learning more about the people you met.
- *Continue exploring the heart dynamics of living on mission with Serge's* The Mission-Centered Life *study.* Written by a former Serge missionary, *The Mission-Centered Life* will help you make connect the spiritual lessons you learned on your trip with the day-to-day realities of living on mission.
- *Learn more about God's plan for global missions and your role in it with Serge's* You are Sent *small group study.* Consider

using it to lead an adult eduction class at your church or in your community.

- *Download Serge's free* **Going Global** *guide which will help you and your church know how to strengthen your involvement in world outreach.* You can get your own copy at serge.org/going-global.
- *Subscribe to Serge's podcast,* **Grace at the Fray,** *to hear more stories of how God is at work to grow his kingdom around the world.* Available anywhere you normally access podcasts or at serge.org/podcast.

Praying

- *Ask to be added to the prayer update lists for missionaries or ministries you encountered on the trip.* Now that you've had a chance to meet them and see what they do, you can pray in deeper ways for them.
- *Sign up for prayer updates from all of the missionaries your church supports.* Even if you haven't met them yet, it's likely that they will visit your church sometime when they're home.
- *If your church doesn't have a system for distributing and updating missionary prayer requests, consider volunteering to start and maintain one.* With a little cutting and pasting, you can help those in your church to see all of the prayer needs in one place.
- *Choose a region of the world that you feel drawn to and become a "prayer expert" on the needs of God's people in that region.* It could be connected to your trip or someplace God has put on your heart. Seeing how God is involved with people from many countries in a particular region of the world is a great way to get a broader perspective on his purposes. Examples could include house churches in China, ministry to North African Muslims, the needs of immigrant communities in Western countries, sex trafficking in Asia, etc.
- *Make it a point to write a personal email to one of the missionaries you met or one that you or your church supports.* Let them know how much you appreciate what they are doing and ask if there are particular ways you can pray for their spiritual

growth. You'd be surprised at how often the spiritual needs of missionaries are overlooked when people ask for a report on their work.

- *Consider using the resources from websites* like Operation World (www.operationworld.org) or the Voice of the Martyrs (www.persecution.com) to gain information about specific countries and prayer needs.
- *No matter what you do, use your own mission trip experience to pray more deeply and personally for people.* Once you've met people serving on the field, it's a lot easier to see missions as a large family of relationships instead of separate ministries and causes.
- *Consider being the "prayer champion" for future short-term teams that your church sends.* Offer to coordinate prayer requests, update your leaders, and recruit others to pray during the trip.

Serving

- *Adopt a missionary or missionary team for a year.* You can do this by yourself, as a family, with friends, or with your small group or Sunday school class. Find out how you can pray for them, but also how you can minister to them and encourage them.
- *Send a care package.* All missionaries have things they like that are almost impossible to get where they live. Food or spices, DVDs, puzzles and games, clothes, high quality tools and repair items—there is always a list of things that will lift a missionary's spirit. Mostly they'll just be grateful that someone back home is thinking of them.
- *Consider serving on your church's missions committee.* Now that you've had a chance to see things firsthand, perhaps you can be of service to the rest of your church by helping them support, stay connected to, and pray for missionaries.
- *Go out of your way to meet the needs of missionaries while at home.* When missionaries are on home assignment or traveling to meet supporters, they often need a whole range of things, from temporary accommodation and transportation, to help

with figuring out schooling options and setting up new cell phones. Tip: contact your missionary and ask specifically what she needs; don't offer a generic "Let me know if I can help."

- *Offer your expertise to missionaries while they are home or on the field.* Are you a whiz with taxes? Run your own IT consulting agency? Know how to research the best digital camera to use in rugged, humid conditions? Inevitably you are good at something that a missionary could use help with. The better you know your missionaries, the more you'll learn how you can help.

- *Donate your air miles to help missionaries get home for special occasions.* One of the hardest things for missionaries is missing important family/life events due to the expense of air travel. Offering extra frequent flier miles, often good for flights, car rental, and lodging, is a tangible way to help.

- *Let a missionary family use your vacation or rental property for free, or donate a week or two at a timeshare you own.* Finding places to just "be away," even when they are home, is a huge need and challenge on a limited budget. Offering missionaries a place to go and rest is a tremendous blessing.

- *Offer to collect and ship needed ministry items to a missionary.* Fifty soccer balls? School supplies? New socks and underwear? You'd be surprised what you'll hear about when you start asking. Even when a missionary has funds for the items, getting them into their country is difficult. Having someone who is willing to help is a huge blessing. Be sure to ask your missionary about any taxes or import duties they may have to pay for goods shipped to them and include that cost in your budget.

Giving

- *Evaluate your monthly giving to missionaries.* Every missionary is in need of monthly supporters. After you have met your giving commitments to your local church, pray about supporting a new missionary or increasing your giving to missionaries you currently support.

- *Evaluate your giving to special projects.* Setting aside money throughout the year or using some of the money from bonuses, tax refunds, or rebates is a great way to bless missionaries with one-time gifts. There are always unexpected expenses on the field, and *you* can be part of God's answer to their prayers.

- *Sponsor a project or give to a missionary as a family.* Getting children involved in learning about missionaries, other countries, and God's kingdom is a great way to introduce them to missions. Children can earn money from chores or through fundraisers to help contribute to your giving.
- *Help your church organize a special giving project for children.* Help your children's Sunday school or VBS program find a way to collect money and give to missions. It could be a project or a missionary, but getting kids involved in giving is a great way to not only help missionaries, but to foster a child's interest in missions.
- *Help your church organize a special project to support.* Find out if one of your missionaries has a special funding need for a particular project. Then offer to organize the youth group to run a fundraising event (a golf outing, bake sale, etc.) to meet that need. This raises needed money and also highlights your ministry partners and their work.
- *Fast for a month!* Relax, you can still eat. Consider giving up one of your little luxuries for a month—your daily latte, that trip through the drive-thru window—and donating the money you save to a missions cause. Every time you'd normally spend that money, it's a good reminder to pray for the people you want to support.
- *Offer to host a support party for a visiting missionary.* Missionaries are regularly in need of opportunities to make new contacts, explain their work, and invite people to join them in prayer and financial support. Be bold and offer to host a party for them. Invite your friends so they'll have a ready and waiting audience.

Going

- *Do everything you can to make sure your pastors can visit mission fields.* Whether it's encouraging them to go, offering to mow their lawn while they're gone, or offering to watch their children so their spouse can join them, regularly having your pastors visit the mission fields you support is an essential part of keeping the vision and passion for missions in front of your congregation.

- *Help your church take its next mission trip.* Offer to help recruit, make a video, invite people to the information sessions, or keep the books for the team. You may not be ready or able to go again, but you can help others get there.

- *Encourage people to go.* Everyone has a million reasons why they haven't taken a mission trip. Help them overcome those reasons by winsomely sharing your own experience.

- *Find internationals living near you and reach out to them.* Often people from countries that are closed—or nearly so—to missionaries are open to talk about spiritual things when they are living away from home. Offer to host a foreign family, invite them over for lunch, help them figure out how to register for the local youth soccer team, or volunteer to teach English.

- *If you have in-demand skills (medical, dental, construction, etc.), consider taking regular trips every year or every other year.* By working with the same group repeatedly, you can minimize time and effort and maximize effects. You can also be a bridge for others with similar skills who don't know how to get involved.

- *Consider going for one to six months.* A week or two is great, but often the needs of the field are better met when you can offer needed services or help for a longer period of time. Many mission agencies can connect you with a team or service area that you have a passion for.

- *Consider going . . . forever!* Not everyone is called to be a missionary. But some are! Maybe as a result of your trip (or a longer stay), you need to set aside time to listen and see if God is calling you to longer service. It's not an "all or nothing" proposition. Take one step at a time and recruit a prayer team to walk with you.

- *If you are thinking about exploring a future in missions, Serge offers missions opportunities all the way from two months to long term.* Find more info at serge.org.

DEBRIEF THREE | THE ONGOING JOURNEY

Timeframe for Completion: Six months after you return

INTRODUCTION

Can you believe that it's been six months since your mission trip? Often the hustle and bustle of daily life can dim our memories of the spiritual lessons and experiences that were crystal clear to us when we first returned.

In the first debrief, we asked you to record some of those experiences and emotions. In the second debrief, we asked you to reflect more deliberately on what God had done and, just as importantly, what he still wanted to do through you to expand his kingdom. This debrief is intended to give you a chance to sit with God and honestly ask, "How is it going? Am I doing the things that I sensed you wanted me to do?"

Don't forget the lessons you learned through the daily devotions—you're no more of a spiritual superstar now than you were on the trip. It's likely that you've had plans you haven't carried out, or you've made mistakes along the way. That's okay. Jesus knows. He's with you. He cares. And he's just as able to use you here and now as he was six months ago on the trip.

1. Review the plan you came up with on page 129 for praying, serving, giving, and going. Then spend a few minutes answering the following questions:

    Praying differently . . .

    How have you been doing with your plans for praying differently?

    ....

    ....

    ....

....

....

Are there items you listed that you still haven't gotten to? If so, can you make some tangible plans right now to get to them?

....

....

....

....

....

Serving more intentionally . . .

How have you been doing with your plans for serving more intentionally?

....

....

....

....

....

Are there items you listed that you still haven't gotten to? If so, can you make some tangible plans right now to get to them?

....

....

....

....

....

Giving more generously . . .

How have you been doing with your plans for giving more generously?

....

....

....

....

....

Are there items you listed that you still haven't gotten to? If so, can you make some tangible plans right now to get to them?

....

....

....

....

....

Going boldly . . .

How have you been doing with your plans for going boldly?

....

....

....

....

....

Are there items you listed that you still haven't gotten to? If so, can you make some tangible plans right now to get to them?

....

....

....

....

....

2. As you have tried to work through your plan, where have you seen it reveal more of your need for Christ? How has God been meeting you in these areas?

....

....

....

....

....

CONCLUSION
Writing the Next Chapter

BY PATRIC KNAAK

At the start of the devotional, I pointed out a simple but startling fact: the *events* of the book of Acts have concluded, but the *story* of Acts continues. It continues around the world, through the lives of God's people as we continue to follow our risen Savior. It continues as we proclaim the good news of his message of salvation. It continues as we love others and work for justice in his name, bearing witness to God's great plan to redeem and renew all things.

In the same way, while the events of your mission trip have ended, the story of your mission trip continues. In fact, learning to live fully engaged in God's mission is one of the primary benefits of taking a few weeks to participate in a short-term experience. While good certainly happens during these weeks, it's what comes after that matters most. As Eric McLaughlin pointed out in his devotion, the book of Acts ends in a very unremarkable manner. I think that's intentional—Luke is reminding us that we carry on the advance of God's kingdom in our normal, everyday lives.

Through your preparation, your devotional time on the field, and your debriefs, I hope that you have started to see your need for Jesus in new and deeper ways. The need for daily dependence on God's Spirit so that you can love and serve others doesn't end now that you are back home. The language, people, food, and culture may now be familiar, but the message of a God who loves you so much that he's willing to die for you should still feel wonderfully alien. Let it catch you off guard and take your breath away when you consider the immense love that God has for you, his beloved child.

Whenever grace moves into our lives, it always moves us beyond ourselves. In your neighborhood and around the world, God is building his kingdom, and your loving Heavenly Father invites you to join him in the family business of redemption and reconciliation. In the years ahead, I hope you'll remember those special days of your mission trip when you stood on the front lines of the kingdom and saw God and yourself more clearly, so that you too will travel the road with Jesus, loving what he loves and wanting what he wants. Where will he lead you? Jesus is writing us into his great story, and the very best is yet to come.

TIPS FOR LEADERS

Leading a short-term trip can be one of the most rewarding and daunting things you'll ever do! While there is no one way to lead a trip well, the following best practices will help you and your team get the most out of your experience.

Familiarize yourself with *Life-Changing Mission* a few months before your trip. Order copies for your whole team and build the price into the cost of the trip instead of asking people to order their own. There are exercises to be done before, during, and after the trip. Knowing what they are will help you integrate them into your plans.

Hold a mandatory pre-trip meeting or two. There will be some logistical details you need to cover, but use these times primarily to start setting the spiritual tone and expectations for the trip. The Before You Go section on page 1 has several exercises for people to complete before the trip starts. Consider using the Inventory of Needs and Hopes on page 6 with your team during one of these meetings. Give them about 10 minutes to complete the exercise and then break up into small groups to discuss their answers and pray for one another.

Set your schedule wisely, ensuring there is enough time each day for individuals to spend time with God using the devotions from *Life-Changing Mission*. While you are on-site, it's tempting to try to fill every minute of the day with work so that you can get the most amount done. While the days may be long and the workload heavy, in our experience it's a mistake not to build *at least* 30 minutes into the daily schedule for personal time with God. If your schedule is tight, you can break it up into 15 minutes in the morning and 15 minutes in the evening. Some of the best things that will come out of your trip will happen as a result of how your people live their lives differently once they return home. Don't short-circuit the time they need to read Scripture, pray, and capture what God is doing in their hearts. If you are working with an outside party for the trip, communicate your desire to them about including devotional time in the schedule as you plan the trip with them.

Anticipate conflict. When it comes to short-term trips, conflict is a given. It may be overt or hidden, but everyone is going to be stretched, stressed, and sleep-deprived. So don't be surprised when divisions arise or harsh words are spoken. Instead, see this as an opportunity for the Holy Spirit to work above and beyond. Listen. Be patient. Exercise kindness and sympathy. Help others listen to one another. Facilitate peacemaking, repentance, and forgiveness. Some of the most lasting lessons from the trip come from having to work out the implications of the gospel together. Back at home, we can just hide and cover it up. Not so on the trip. Take advantage of this.

Be prepared for spiritual warfare. Satan will not be happy about your trip and will do practically anything he can to derail you, your team, and your work. Don't let this scare you or surprise you. Jesus has overcome Satan, and he will be with you. Instead, use God's Word powerfully to uncover Satan's lies, and maintain your spiritual connection with Jesus. This is part of the reason why individual and group prayer is so important.

Make practical preparations with the assumption that things will go wrong. No matter how well you plan, things always go awry. Carry paper backups of important documents, travel plans, addresses, and phone numbers. Know how to contact your home country's embassy if you are traveling overseas. Bring extra cash and keep it hidden. Be sure to bring extra over-the-counter medication for headaches, travel sickness, and digestive complaints. In some cases, you may want to ask your doctor about bringing extra medicine for digestive disorders or infections. Don't skip updating your immunizations. Make sure that someone who is not going on the trip knows where you will be at all times and prearrange check-in times with them. An ounce of prevention is worth a pound of cure when you miss a connection, lose your phone or laptop with key information stored on it, or have your wallet stolen. When things do go wrong, remember: you have a Father in heaven who loves you and who is in charge. He'll help you and take care of you. Your travel may take longer or you may not get all of the activities done that you planned to do, but it will still be OK.

Learn to love the people you are coming to serve. Try not to spend all your time exclusively as a team. Invite local missionaries or national partners to join you for prayer and meals. If your schedule allows, get out and experience your host culture. See if you can strike up a conversation with nationals, and if you can, listen 80 percent of the time. God loves everyone, and every culture reflects his glory in various ways. Take advantage of being out of your cultural bubble to see, taste, and experience an entirely different way of life.

Plan to use the three debrief exercises extensively with your team. One of the unique features of *Life-Changing Mission* are the debrief exercises on page 121. In fact, they may be the most valuable part of the devotional because they are designed to help your team take the amazing things they will see God do during your trip and reshape the trajectory of their lives once they return back home. No matter what you are able to accomplish on your trip or how mightily God uses you, it will pale in comparison to living a life fully engaged in living on mission once you return home.

- *Debrief One* should be completed at the end of your trip—on your way home or in the first week after you get back at the latest. You want people to capture memories and how they saw God work while it is still fresh in their minds. Build some time into your schedule to do this if at all possible.
- *Debrief Two* should be completed four to six weeks after you return home. Consider using it as part of your team reunion dinner when everyone will be sharing pictures, reflecting on what they've seen and heard, and integrating the lessons they've learned with the challenges of their daily lives.
- *Debrief Three* is designed to do six months after you return. Send out some friendly email reminders and make a point to follow up personally with each member of your team over coffee or a meal to hear about their plans from the third debrief section. The memories of their trip will fade, but the impact doesn't have to. In fact, their experience on the trip will hopefully fuel a whole new level of engagement with missions as they give, go, or send others.

ACKNOWLEDGMENTS

Content creation at Serge is always a bit of a team effort. Nowhere has that been more true than with *Life-Changing Mission*. We are profoundly grateful to all of our missionaries who contributed content to this project. Their wisdom and experience has made the devotions immeasurably richer.

Thanks also to Barbara Miller Juliani and the whole team at New Growth Press. Without their encouragement to do a follow-up to Serge's original short-term devotional, *On Mission: Devotions for Your Short-Term Trip*, we'd have never found the space and time to bring the idea to reality.

Finally, our deepest thanks to Aislinn Meyer who joined Serge's Renewal Team in the US after spending many years overseas as a missionary and church planter. Her organizational, creative, and editorial skills were essential to crafting the final product you now see. It is not an overstatement to say that without her, we would have never gotten *Life-Changing Mission* across the finish line.

MEET THE AUTHORS

Emily Shrader serves as a Renewal Specialist for Serge. She and her husband, David, and their three children, Mae, Wesley, and Miriam, served with Serge in North Africa for more than a decade. Emily has a bachelor's degree in biblical and theological studies and youth ministry from Gordon College and has studied biblical counseling with the Christian Counseling and Educational Foundation. Before leaving for the field, Emily worked in youth and campus ministry, participated in Community Bible Study leadership, and partnered with David as he pastored a small inner-city church in Pittsburgh. While in North Africa, Emily worked alongside David as he pastored an international fellowship and trained local pastors. She and her family currently reside in Goldsboro, NC, where her husband David serves as a chaplain in the USAF.

Eric and Rachel McLaughlin both grew up all across the United States. They met during medical school and were both interested in international long-term missions. They were married in 2005, then in 2007, while Rachel was completing her residency in OB-GYN and Eric in family practice in Ann Arbor, MI, they joined up with two other medical families from their church and decided to pursue medical missions as a community. They went together to Tenwek Hospital in Kenya from 2009–2011, where they added a few team members and decided to pursue long-term work in Burundi. They joined Serge in 2011, before attending French language school for a year and arriving in Burundi in the summer of 2013. They live at Kibuye Hope Hospital in the impoverished rural interior of Burundi, in the heart of central Africa, where they care for patients while training national doctors as professors for Hope Africa University, a Christian Burundian University. They have the distinction of having three children born on three continents. Maggie was born in 2009 in Michigan, Ben was born in 2011 in Kenya, and Toby was born in 2013 in France.

Jennifer Myhre serves as Serge's Area Director for Central and East Africa along with her husband and best friend, Scott, who is also a medical doctor. She holds an MD and a Master's in Public Health from Johns Hopkins University and has served for over three decades as a pediatrician in Uganda and Kenya. Jennifer combines curative and preventive care by working in local hospitals, participating in health management, and promoting community health, focusing in the areas of HIV prevention, newborn survival, and childhood nutrition. She and Scott have invested heavily in the training of local doctors and nurses, conducting research to better understand and address health issues in their area, and being the hands of Jesus in the hardest places. They have four adult children that were raised in Africa and for whom *The Rwendigo Tales* books were written as Christmas presents.

Jeremy Sink graduated from Reformed Theological Seminary and served for ten years as a church planter and pastor in the Piedmont Triad region of NC. There, God opened his eyes to the need for experienced pastors to help plant new churches among the Japanese, where less than one percent of the population is Christian. He moved to Japan in 2012 with his wife Gina and their three children, Joshua, Josiah, and Garrett. They work closely with an international church plant called All Nations Fellowship, where Jeremy currently serves as the lead pastor. Additionally, the Sinks are involved in mentoring and training young church planters and Christian leaders through partnerships with Christ Bible Institute and the Church Planting Institute of Japan. The work is hard, but the Sinks are encouraged by how the Spirit is working in Nagoya.

Josiah Bancroft is originally from Birmingham, Alabama, and his wife, Barbara, comes from Jacksonville, Florida; they were married in 1975. Josiah is an ordained minister in the Presbyterian Church in America, and together they have planted churches in Louisiana and Alabama. Josiah and Barbara worked overseas in Ireland and stateside with Serge from 1992–2004. They left Serge for five years in 2005 for Josiah to serve as a pastor at Grace Community in Asheville, NC. They returned to Serge in 2011 for Josiah to serve as the Senior Director of Mission, a role in which he served until 2023. He now serves as a Senior Advisor for Serge, mentors leaders, and helps create gospel-centered, mission-engaged content.

Lindsay has served in Europe with Serge since 2012. She is passionate about evangelism and enjoys participating in church-planting work among the least-reached peoples of the world. Due to the sensitive nature of her work, we are limiting her biographical information.

Marc Davis grew up at New Life Church in Jenkintown, Pennsylvania, in the years when Serge (formerly World Harvest Mission) was being launched. During those years, he saw people being transformed by the gospel of grace, and that same grace got hold of him too. Marc and his wife Susan met at the University of Virginia and married in 1992. After three years on Intervarsity staff, he completed an MDiv from Westminster Seminary in 1997. Marc is an ordained minister in the Presbyterian Church in America and served on the pastoral staff at New Life Church Glenside for twelve years. Marc joined Serge's Renewal team in 2019 as Global Learning Program Leader and now serves as Serge's Associate Director of Renewal. In that role, he is excited to see missionaries, pastors, and others involved in ministry empowered by the gospel to live lives of great freedom in dependence on Jesus for everything. Marc and Susan have three children: Nathaniel, Maggie, and Owen.

Patric Knaak serves as Deputy Director of Mission, supporting the growth and effectiveness of Serge's overall mission work. Previously he served as Serge's Area Director for Renewal from 2007–2023, stewarding and shepherding the teams that teach, write, train, and mentor for Serge. He served for many years as the pastor for discipleship at Naperville Presbyterian Church and is an ordained minister in the Presbyterian Church in America. He is the author of *On Mission: Devotions for your Short-Term Trip* and coauthor of *Psalms: Real Prayers for Real Life*. His studies have included theology and New Testament at Moody Bible Institute, Wheaton Graduate School, and New College, University of Edinburgh. He lives near Serge's home office with his wife Jennifer and their son Parker. He enjoys travel, vintage fountain pens, dark chocolate, and BBQ.

Wade Savant and his wife Aly married in Memphis in 2013. The Savants spent their first year of marriage working as missionaries in La Paz, Bolivia. During that time, they felt the Lord's call to return to the US so Wade could pursue an MDiv at Reformed Theological Seminary in Charlotte, North Carolina, where he graduated in 2017. While in Charlotte they sensed the Lord reaffirm their desire to return to international ministry with a special emphasis on seeing the local church grow and flourish in spiritually adverse cultures. They moved to Prague, Czech Republic, in 2018 where Wade served for four years as a pastor at Faith Community Church and Aly worked to disciple Czech and expat women. They also served for a year in Scotland, encouraging and equipping Scottish pastors and their wives. Wade now serves in pastoral ministry in the US. The Savants have two sweet kids, Everett and Lena.

mission
propelled by God's Grace

Go and grow with us.

Since 1983, Serge has been helping individuals and churches engage in global mission. From short-term trips to long-term missions – we want to see the power of God's grace transform your own life and motivate and sustain you to move into the lives of others – particularly those who do not yet know Jesus.

As a sending agency we:

- **Take a gospel-centered approach to life and ministry**
- **Provide proactive Missionary Care**
- **Practice incarnational ministry**
- **Believe God works in our weakness**

Visit us online at:
serge.org/missions

Grace at the Fray

Gospel Renewal
fuels mission

Serge is...

As an international missions agency, we realize we need the grace of the gospel in our own lives, even as we take the message of God's grace to others. Our work consists of helping people experience on-going *gospel renewal* and equipping them to move outward into *mission*.

We seek to foster this transformation in ministry leaders, churches, and all believers around the world.

Visit us online at:
serge.org

MISSIONS | MENTORING | RESOURCES

Grace at the Fray

resources

for continued spiritual growth

We never outgrow our need for the gospel.

No matter where you are on your Christian journey, Serge resources help you live out the gospel in every part of your life and encourage the same growth in others. Whether you are a church leader, actively engaged in ministry, or just seeking to go deeper in your relationship with God - we have resources that can help.

- **Books and Studies**
- **Discipleship and Training**
- **Grace-Centered Teaching Events**
- **Webinars**
- **Podcast**

Visit us online at:
serge.org/renewal

Grace at the Fray